PREACHING FROM THE PEW

Preaching from the Pew
A Message for the Church

PATRICIA G. BROWN

Geneva Press
Louisville, Kentucky

Unless otherwise indicated scripture quotations are from the
New Revised Standard Version of the Bible, copyright © 1989
by the Division of Christian Education of the National Council
of the Churches of Christ in the U.S.A., and are used by permission.

Verses marked TLB are taken from *The Living Bible* © 1971.
Used by permission of Tyndale House Publishers, Inc., Wheaton, IL 60189.

For information, address Geneva Press,
100 Witherspoon Street, Louisville, Kentucky 40202-1396.

Book and cover design by Jennifer K. Cox
Cover photograph by Richard Brasington

Published by Geneva Press
Louisville, Kentucky

This book is printed on acid-free paper that meets the
American National Standards Institute Z39.48 standard. ∞

PRINTED IN THE UNITED STATES OF AMERICA
98 99 00 01 02 03 04 05 06 07 — 10 9 8 7 6 5 4 3 2 1

Library of Congress Cataloging-in-Publication Data

Brown, Patricia G., date.
    Preaching from the pew : a message for the church / Patricia
G. Brown. — 1st ed.
        p.   cm.
    ISBN 0-664-50019-6 (alk. paper)
    1. Presbyterian Church—Sermons. 2. Sermons, American.
I. Title.
BX9178.B7424P74   1988   97-47075
252′.051—dc21

Contents

Part IV.
Up Close and Personal with God:
Our Personal Relationship with God

Part V.
When Faith Goes Public: Issues of Social Concern

Preface

It is a rare Sunday that one of us sitting in the pew can change places with one of those who usually stands behind the pulpit. And on such rare Sundays, those of us who are not accustomed to the pulpit tend to be concerned that we will speak unwisely or say something in error or misinterpret scripture or some other terrible thing which will make the preacher sorry that he or she ever asked us in the first place.

Fortunately, those churches in the Presbytery of Cincinnati who have asked me have been very gracious. I have delighted in these special opportunities to speak from my heart, to share from my experience of life, to unravel the who of me and the what of my relationship with God.

It is with pleasure that I have put together some of my sermons and meditations for others to ponder. With a little help from my friends—Deb Ramey, Marybeth Kantner, Richard Brasington, and Bea Conner—and my son Erik, I self-produced the first edition. It was so well received that Geneva Press has agreed to publish *Preaching from the Pew* again so that those of you who know me and know of me as Moderator of the 209th General Assembly of the Presbyterian Church (U.S.A.), 1997, will have the chance to journey along with me in this volume.

It is my hope that coming to know of my experience will add a new depth of understanding to your experience as the reader. For that reason, space has been provided among these pages to encourage you to record your thoughts together with mine "In Your Own Words."

May God's grace and peace be with us on the journey.

Patricia G. Brown

PART I.

Let Us Worship God:
Issues of Faith and Worship

The Beloved Community

Psalm 107:23–43 and 1 Peter 5:1–11

I must have been about three or four years old. It was the first Sunday of the month and therefore Communion Sunday at Grace United Presbyterian Church. Huddled between my mother and my grandmother in our usual place—the second pew from the front on the left—I sucked my thumb and counted the straight-backed chairs that were lined up facing the congregation. There were thirteen of them and they were separated into two groups by a heavy table covered with a crisp white cloth.

When the minister sat in a chair next to the table, I became aware of soft organ music in the background. It was "Let us break bread together . . . on our knees" and everybody started to sing when twelve men in dark suits marched stiffly up the center aisle to fill the twelve remaining chairs. My grandfather was among those men and I tried to get his attention so that we could exchange winks like we always did. But this time he knotted his brows and shook his head slightly. Instantly I realized that this was something very special and very serious.

When the last moans from the organ—"Oh-h-h-h Lord have mer-r—r-cy on me" hung like a whisper above our heads, the minister rose to his feet. Beautiful words in mystical rhythms tumbled from his lips as he broke a loaf of bread in his hands and held a cup with a silver stem up for all to see. He

3

gave six of the men shiny trays filled with delicate white wafers to pass out to the congregation and to the other six he gave heavy trays with lots of miniature glasses filled to the brim.

When I heard about "the angels, the archangels, and all the company of heaven," I longed to be a part of the magic. I was too young for the wine and the wafer, so I settled for a large black button popped into my mouth and closed my eyes as I had seen my grandmother do. And then it happened. The magic came. I felt warm all over. I felt like I belonged to something wonderful—something like my parents and grand-parents—but much, much bigger.

What are your earliest recollections of church?

I was at a meeting of the Stewardship and Communication Ministry Unit of the General Assembly when this question was asked to help us get to know each other. The stories around the room were varied and fascinating. Many of the committee members had recollections from childhood, but there were also those who came to the church as teens and adults.

The one story that I remember most vividly was that of a brilliant woman who happens to be legally blind. Her family decided to stop going to church when she was born because they were embarrassed and afraid of ridicule. Church was not something one discussed openly at home, but her friends at school often spoke of Sunday school or church activities. By the time she reached adolescence, her curiosity was at its peak. One weekend, after spending the night with a friend, she had the opportunity to go to church and she jumped at the chance even though her friend was somewhat reluctant. She loved the chance—the music, the friendliness. People really seemed to care about her, enough so that she returned again and again.

In Psalm 107 we find two groups of people. The first group made their livelihoods from the sea. Together they experi-enced a raging storm, together they sought God's help, and together they found peace in the heaven of God. The second group came together because they were hungry. Separating themselves from the wicked whom God had punished with famine, they came together to work the soil and raise cattle. They, too, were protected by God, who the psalmist says "raises them from distress and makes their families like flocks"—like a community. So how is this relevant to us? First we learn that experience is the key to how we understand and appreciate community. We experience community and it is that experience that determines what community means to us.

Our first biblical group experienced danger and were rescued as a community. The second experienced cooperation and were successful as a community. My recollection of church was the experience of belonging to a community. My friend's experience was the discovery of acceptance and love by a community of people.

But we can have a community experience at a football game or a neighborhood picnic. What separates community in the secular sense from the community of faith—the beloved community?

All Christians participate in the experience of the Lord's Supper. As a matter of fact, Paul uses the Greek word *koinonia* to refer to both communion and community. *Koinonia* concentrates our attention on personal relationships, on the ways we are there for one another, on the quality of our concern for one another. Michael Kinnamon of the Lexington Theological Seminary in Kentucky says, "We have communion with one another because we have communion with a common savior and are, therefore, related to one another by blood—the blood of Christ." Now there's a powerful thought. Everyone and anyone who shares the body of Jesus Christ in the sacrament of Holy Communion becomes blood sisters and brothers with everyone else who comes to that table.

If you remember going through the seriousness and ceremony of making some childhood friend a blood sister or brother, you can understand the kind of commitment to each other that is inherent in such a relationship. Think of the impact that kind of commitment could have on you as a member of the church, as a Presbyterian, as a citizen of the world!

Such a notion of commitment to each other for the sake of the other's fulfillment is a wonderful new vision of community that could truly make a difference. It would include love for those who are not lovable in the eyes of the world. It would depend on forgiveness—a covenant with God to restore broken relationships, to forgive debts, to oppose oppression, and to seek God's peace together. How can we begin to build such a beloved community? Why not begin with your own congregation? After all, it is the congregation where people shape the church and are shaped by it. With the installation of a new pastor, for instance, a church is in a perfect position to begin thinking old thoughts in new ways.

Let me unpack that notion so you can see what it would look like. Members would have a sense of mutual obligation with each other and the pastor. They would all share their talents and resources with others. They would find new meaning in their membership and everyone would be loved even when they "didn't deserve it." The beloved community continually reforms itself to seek the good of the whole. It is proud of itself and its accomplishments. It does not fall apart when it faces problems and difficulties. However, that's not all God wants of us. Yes, as Peter (1 Peter 5:1–11) says, it is up to us "to tend the flock of God that is in your charge, exercising the oversight, not under compulsion but willingly, as God would have you do it . . ." (v. 2).

I think God wants us to be more than chaplains of the status quo. I think that at the same time God is calling us to be the beloved community, God is asking that we act faithfully in the world's ambiguous environment. Every member of the beloved community stands on the front line of a battle against decaying family structures, lost values, distrust, and the "me-ism" that plagues our society. We are asked to become stronger and more relevant in a time when our relevancy is most challenged.

It is not easy for today's Christians to face these new gladiators. It is not easy for the beloved community not to be devoured by today's lions in the current coliseum of life. But the scripture says, "Resist him, steadfast in your faith, for you know that your brothers and sisters in all the world are undergoing the same kinds of suffering" (v. 9).

We can do it. We can be reconciled to one another. We can act with Christian responsibility in a world of complacency. We have a new vision of the beloved community—a vision based on a covenant with God to live as a community of faith, because through Christ we have a new relationship with one another and with God.

"The God of all grace, who has called us to his eternal glory in Christ, will himself restore, support, strengthen, and establish you. To him be the power forever and ever" (1 Peter 5:10b–11).

Gracious God and Nurturing Spirit,
We are many voices striving to tell your story.
We are many lives swimming against the current to
witness for you.
Though our ways may be different, help us to come
together as shepherds and flock to share ourselves
with friends and strangers in your name.
Teach us to talk and listen, laugh and cry, argue and differ,
choose and decide, work and worship—as one body,
the body of Christ.
Create us, your beloved community, to laud and glorify you for
ever and ever. Amen.

In Your Own Words

Living in the Discomfort Zone

Exodus 1:8–14 and Romans 12:1–8

Sometimes life is a rocking chair on the front porch. We are constantly in motion but our lives are basically the same from day to day. Then, wham, something grabs us from behind and plunges us spinning and whirling into a deep, dark hole called the unknown.

Sometimes the thing that grabs us is the death of someone we love, someone like a spouse or a beloved pastor. Sometimes the thing is a natural disaster like a tornado that barrels through and leaves us without a place to live, clothes to wear, or food to eat. Sometimes it is a disease or a disability or a quirk of fate that changes the way we live or relate to each other.

Sometimes the thing is a life circumstance of poverty, oppression, racism, sexism, displacement, unemployment, aging, marital discord—the list goes on. For whatever reason, we are no longer able to fight the fight, find the rainbow, keep on with the keeping on.

The dark hole of not knowing what to do or whether we will survive to see the light of a new day is a scary place. Cold, confused, and perhaps frustrated, we spend a lot of time and energy feeling sorry for ourselves because we are suffering and suffering is not comfortable. Through no fault of our own, we find ourselves in the Discomfort Zone.

In the book of Exodus (1:8–14) we find the people of Jacob still in Egypt, but long after the "good ol' days" which Joseph had arranged. Almost three hundred years have passed. The pharaohs never heard of somebody named Joseph. The Hyksos pharaohs who had favored Joseph were foreigners to Egypt and had been driven off by this time. The upper and lower kingdoms had been reunited and the country was at the height of its military power. New pharaohs ruled from Thebes and Memphis, but attention was again focused on the rich and fertile region at the delta of the Nile River.

Exodus opens with the accession of Sethos I, who has the grand idea to build large cities where supplies can be stored. He is the developer of the plan and Rameses II—played by Yul Brynner in the movie *The Ten Commandments*—is to complete the plan when he succeeds Sethos.

Now Sethos is not too comfortable with all these non-Egyptians living in the area. Like the Latinos and Chicanos that live along the borders in the United States, they had strange customs, they looked different, they probably spoke in a different language. Plus, there were so many of them that sheer numbers posed a threat. Who knew what they might do?

Sethos decided he could keep the aliens under control and build his cities at the same time. He would simply work them to death. And so the great building projects of the new kingdom of Egypt were begun with Hebrews digging out the mud, making the bricks, and dragging the stones. However, the plan doesn't work. The cities are built, but the Jews multiply instead of decreasing, because God wants to build the nation of Israel and has promised fruitfulness to the chosen since Adam, Noah, Abraham, Isaac, and Jacob.

Infuriated, the Egyptians become "ruthless in imposing tasks" and "made their lives bitter with hard service." Things were so bad that Jews still commemorate their "bitter lives" in the Passover meal that is eaten with "bitter herbs."

I moved to Cincinnati twenty-two years ago with two children—a son in kindergarten and a younger son in the Infant

Stimulation Program at Stepping Stones Center for the Handicapped. Ivan's program at Stepping Stones was in the morning and Erik's half day of kindergarten was in the afternoon. Erik and I ate in route, but Ivan required more assistance. Despite his brain damage and cerebral palsy, Ivan was hyperactive—constantly on the move even when restrained. He never learned how to talk or to use the toilet, but he could strip down to the "bare" essentials in a heartbeat.

It seemed that I was constantly feeding or cleaning people up, and when I wasn't doing that I was behind the wheel. I barely knew anyone, Erik was continually demanding the attention I felt I had to give to Ivan before he hurt himself, and my husband was always on the road building shopping centers. It seemed like things would never change; nothing would be left of me for me.

Whenever there was time to think, I spent it on feeling sorry for myself. I filled every nook and cranny of my being with anger, resentment, and depression. It was just as difficult for me to understand why God had placed this yoke on my shoulders as it is to make sense out of God's choosing the Jews to be a special nation but allowing them to suffer so much.

Second Corinthians 1 offers what I call the "dynamic of extremes." There we find "the God of all consolation, who consoles us in all our affliction, so that we may be able to console those who are in any affliction. . . . For just as the sufferings of Christ are abundant for us, so also our consolation is abundant through Christ" (vv. 3–5).

In other words, how can we understand comfort without knowing suffering? How can we appreciate the sacrifice that Christ made for us? How can we know to comfort others? The more we suffer, the more we are comforted—the ultimate comfort being new life in the resurrection of Jesus Christ.

In my own life, I was to join with the mothers in the waiting area at Stepping Stones to form a grassroots support group that became the Mothers of Special Children. It was my task to develop a program that linked mothers recently learning of a child's disability to experienced mothers whose children had similar disabilities and challenges. It was out of my own "aloneness" that I could understand the feelings of others and offer assistance. The Mothers of Special Children is still very much alive and continues to be available to those who need its comfort.

The suffering of the Hebrews under Egyptian domination standardized the term "comfort" as Israel's hope of the coming of God's kingdom. In fact, Paul makes the word *comfort* synonymous to God's deliverance.

In *Unexpected News* (Westminster Press, 1984, 39), a book that looks at the Bible through third world eyes, Robert McAfee Brown, takes special note of the story of Exodus. He says, "We have seen enough to secure the main lines of the exodus story: in a situation of oppression . . . God takes sides . . . with the oppressed . . . to free them from oppression . . . by empowering them to share in the liberation struggle. The rest is footnotes."

As Presbyterians, we, like the Hebrews of Exodus, are a chosen people.

In preparation for my bid to become Moderator of the General Assembly of the Presbyterian Church (U.S.A.) in 1997, I studied the principles peculiar to the Reformed Faith, those icons of belief that make us witness for Jesus Christ as Presbyterians. The main themes of the Presbyterian Church are referred to as the "Essential Tenants of the Reformed Faith" and there are ten of them.

The first two are universal for all Christians—the mystery of the Trinity and the Incarnation, or God's word made flesh in Jesus Christ. The next two are gleaned from the Protestant Reformation—justification by faith (we don't have to earn forgiveness) and scripture as the final authority for salvation.

In addition to God's sovereignty, faithful stewardship of

God's creation, the sin of idolatry, and seeking justice, the last six tenets include the principles of election and covenant, which both have bearing on our conversation today.

God has elected us for salvation and service. Because we are chosen, we are special, our lives have meaning. We have been saved because God has a purpose for our lives. It is our responsibility to see that God's will is done. How? We prayerfully listen for the cues. We accept our gifts and talents. We act on our convictions. We don't worry about what somebody else is supposed to be doing. We don't have time, because we are busy pursuing our particular responsibilities in service to the kingdom. We walk eagerly in the direction God has called us without giving in to excuses, without avoiding that which may make us uncomfortable, without putting off that which must be done, without refusing to do that which we have been equipped to do. We believe we are saved and we believe we have been saved for a reason.

As Presbyterians, we also believe that God chose us to be in covenant with each other. Because God has chosen us all, we are in this business of promoting the kingdom of God together. Each with particular gifts and designated responsibilities, we depend on God and we need each other. We need God and we depend on the God that is in each of us. We are in an agreement with God and each other to work together. That is why we are chosen for this day and this place and this task. This is what we are supposed to do.

In Romans (12:1–8) Paul uses the metaphor of the human body to illustrate and emphasize the notion of unity within diversity. A foot separated from a leg has no function. A leg separated from a body has no purpose. But Paul also cautions that no one purpose is more important than another. Since the power to give gifts and talents belongs to God, it doesn't matter who gets them or what they are. There is no basis for superior attitudes or self-righteousness when doing the work of the kingdom. Actually, reality is a matter of perception. What one person may perceive as cruel control may be seen as tough love by another. What one person may interpret as restrictive or unnecessary, another may define as stabilization or purging.

It is precisely because reality is as it is perceived that our focus must center on the power which is God. Hence "bad" is "bad" only when it is allowed to take priority over what is good in the mind of the individual, or the "body" of individuals. In Romans, Paul wants the church in Rome to understand how to change their perception, how to prophesy in proportion to their faith. Perhaps we, too, can learn how to change our focus and thereby change what is real.

In the movie *Grand Canyon*, Danny Glover's character was able to deal with the trials of his own life, the senseless suffering of those around him, and the ethos of hopelessness that could have destroyed him by putting it all into perspective. When he considered the wonder of the Grand Canyon, he was able to appreciate himself and his world as a tiny part of the mystery of God's magnificent creations and God's everlasting eternity. We too have a capacity for great faith.

Consider this: What would happen if Presbyterians were to stop angrily second-guessing recent history and consider the work and witness that can take place in the community? Suppose church leaders did not talk about their rough times in angry tones but listened for guidance to conquer new challenges? Wouldn't that alter the current reality? Certainly, we would not be buzzing about the "trouble" in a church, but about the awesomeness of a congregation's spirit in spite of the challenges that have plagued it. The current reality would be different because there would be no reason for it to be the same.

Paul says do not conform to this world but be transformed to something better. Find new life in the Holy Spirit. Reject "ritual" in favor of spiritual acts that incorporate your heart, mind, and will. Worship in obedient service by using your God-given gifts to do the tasks which God has assigned to you. When we put this piece of advice in juxtaposition with Paul's ongoing ability to survive severe beatings, jail, and hunger, not to mention constant criticism, isolation, grief, and resentment, we can put ourselves back into perspective.

Next to the Grand Canyon our troubles are merely loose stones tumbling a few inches down a mountainside. Paul says, "I consider that the sufferings of this present time are not worth comparing with the glory about to be revealed to us" (Rom. 8:18).

In the summer of 1996, I sat in Olympic Stadium on a hot Atlanta, Georgia, night. Already damp with sweat from the long walk from where the car had to be parked and the extra lap around the stadium to find the assigned seats, I wondered at the wisdom of the slacks I was wearing and how long it would take to get something to drink. Unlike the Olympic events of the weeks before, the crowd for the Opening Ceremonies of the Paralympics seemed spread out and I hoped the empty craters of seats would not deter the people who had come to compete.

And then the fireworks went off, an American bald eagle soared over our heads, and a man with no legs parachuted from somewhere in the sky and landed on the field as other members of his squadron followed in dramatic succession. The parade of athletes from 102 countries filled the field and included people who have cerebral palsy, are deaf, or considered legally blind, as well as those who are physically challenged.

I was so struck by what it must have taken for each of them to get to the international competition in Atlanta—especially those from third world countries—that for over two hours I waved to each one that passed by. Those without hands and arms to wave back responded with glowing expressions of appreciation and excitement. Those who could not see could hear the roars of enthusiasm from an ever-growing crowd and they too glowed.

My own lungs ached with Master of Ceremonies Christopher Reeve's every breath of oxygen. My heart pounded when the flame runner with one leg flew up the aisle next to us taking two steps at a time. I could hardly breathe when the flame made its final ascent between the stubbed legs of a man who had scaled Mount Everest. This remarkable athlete made his way to the top of the Olympic torch on a rope, one powerful pull after another. There was no mistaking the collective sigh and cheer that went up when that torch ignited. No one in the now filled-to-capacity stadium of 85,000 people could escape the sense of pride that transformed the road of gloom into the highway of glory.

O Perfect God,
We are amazed at the many examples you use
  to show us the way.
We ask only that we may always
see your light and recognize what you would
  have us do.
Continue to guide our thoughts and our
  spirit on the highway to your glory.
In Jesus' name we pray.
Amen.

In Your Own Words

Living Thank-You Lives

Haggai 2:1–9; Matthew 6:19–21 and 25:14–30

I grew up in Baltimore, and when I was somewhere around six or seven years old, the University of Maryland gave my mother a grant to attend New York University Graduate School rather than the segregated University of Maryland. Since my father was in Korea and my mother was away every weekend, I spent a great deal of time with my grandmother.

My grandmother, Malinda Wheeler Wyatt, believed in the old stream of the reformed faith where things like dancing, playing cards, or going to the movies on Sunday were the epitome of sin. Sunday dinner was always prepared on Saturday, and Sunday afternoons were spent visiting the shut-ins or driving by the movies to look at the sinners. The religion I learned at my grandmother's knee was serious and not to be questioned.

I will never forget the first Sunday she decided that I should put something in the offering plate. She pressed two well-worn nickels into my hand and charged me to hold on to them tightly so I could give them to God when the men came to take up the collection. I was not to play with the nickels or drop them on the floor because they would make a lot of noise and disturb people when they were trying to listen to the preacher.

I remember sitting very still and straight with my fingers tightly wrapped around my new grown-up responsibility. But somewhere in the middle of Reverend Colbert's sermon, I had to open my hand to see if those nickels were okay all squeezed up like that.

In those days, ten cents could buy two large dill pickles or a Hershey's chocolate bar or a whole roll of candy dots or chewy wax figures with colorful, sweet liquid inside. I thought about all the possibilities as I stared down at those ill-fated coins, now moist from the sweat of my tightly clenched fist. There were probably hundreds and hundreds of little children giving pennies and nickels to God all over the world. Would God even notice if I slipped one into my little patent leather purse?

I glanced over at my grandmother. She was involved with the sermon, but her head turned and she warned me to be still with her eyes. I quickly closed my hand back over those nickels. Even if God couldn't tell the difference, my grandmother sure would.

When the men in the dark suits came down the aisles in choreographed precision, I dropped my money into the shiny brass plate and heard them make clinking noises against the side. My grandmother smiled and patted my arm.

As we stood up to sing, I wondered how the men were going to get the money to God. I pictured coins and dollar bills levitating to the heavens but decided that was highly unlikely. Sinners would probably pull them out of the air on the way up. I became so obsessed with the question of logistics that I couldn't wait until after church to find out. I tugged at my grandmother's arm. "How is God going to get the money?" I whispered.

"He already has it," said my grandmother. "He always did."

Haggai, the prophet, would agree: "The silver is mine, and the gold is mine, says the Lord of hosts" (Hag. 2:8).

The confusion is one of direction. We don't give to God, who can "shake the heavens and the earth so that the treasure of all nations will come to fill the church with splendor."

Rather God has given us money, talent, and a world in which to live. Our task is not to pay back, but—as the parable of the talents illustrates—our task is to expand, improve, and build on what is already there.

And how blessed we are! We get to live in the United States of America where we can concern ourselves with how well our meat is inspected, and not in Russia or Zaire where there is no meat to inspect.

We get to live in the United States of America where we can argue about how to make health care affordable, and not in the Sudan where health care barely exists.

We get to live in the United States of America where automatic sprinklers water lawns even when it's raining, and not in Bosnia where people are killed as they try to find water for their families to drink.

God has entrusted us with much, and where much is given much is expected. Living "thank-you lives" is a way to honor that responsibility. And how do we live "thank-you lives"?

I think we already have a pretty good understanding about using our talents to further the kingdom and being good stewards of time. We are almost obsessed with healthy ways of treating the physical bodies we live in and we have even come to understand the need to care for our environment— to conserve and recycle. The part that gets fuzzy is when we start talking about money—dollars—cold, hard cash.

I am reminded of the story of a man who walked into a Mercedes Benz dealership dressed to beat the band. He paraded through the showroom and stopped in front of a beautiful shiny red sports model. Ceremoniously, he passed his hand over the fender, kicked at the white-walled tires and peered inside. The luxurious leather seats pleased his eye and the wonderful dials and gauges intrigued his mind.

A smiling salesperson appeared from nowhere. She invited him to sit inside and get the feel of the vehicle. When he did, his imagination soared. He envisioned himself riding through his neighborhood. People waved in admiration and he felt special.

"How much does this baby cost?" he asked as casually as possible.

The expression on the face of the salesperson changed abruptly. "Sir," she said, "if you have to ask, you can't afford it!"

Will we ever be able to afford true discipleship if we must continuously ask how much it is going to cost?

Following Christ is a beautiful and special experience that can be expensive in many ways. Are we dressing for the part, but unwilling to pay the price? Do we do our good deeds in full view of as many people as possible and carefully seal only our small change in our offering envelopes? Do we base our pledges to the church on how much we think is appropriate or how much the church must have to function and grow? Do we expect all of the pomp and none of the circumstances?

The sports car does indeed have a price. Whether it is posted on the windshield or tucked away in the dealer's note-book, there is a rock-bottom figure that the dealer will accept. Does God have a rock-bottom price for discipleship? How much room is there for negotiation?

Suppose the salesperson had said, "If you love this car as much as you say you do, you can pay me whatever you think it is worth."

How would our buyer have come up with a price? How would you come up with a price?

Would you arrive at a figure by comparing the cost of other vehicles? Would you pay the same thing your cousin Harry paid? What about the amount you paid for your last car? Would you consider how well the car is made, how it makes you feel, or would you attempt to get away with the lowest amount your conscience would allow? What criteria would *you* use to determine its worth?

We belong to the Presbyterian Church because we believe in its style of worship and witness to Christ. We belong to the Presbyterian Church because we find solace, hope, and a sense of family among the members of the congregation.

Conversely, our congregation belongs to us because God provided it for us. Beyond the intimacy of the congregation, there is the presbytery, where pastors are cared for and where struggling congregations can find expertise and financial assistance.

Beyond the family of the presbytery is the synod, where ministries to minorities find direction and where new church developments are envisioned. Beyond the cloister of the synod is the kinship of the General Assembly, where resources are developed, where ministers are matched with congregations, and where Presbyterian stewardship unites to support national and overseas ministries.

God has asked us to manage all this without giving it a price tag. Now it is up to us to handle the monthly maintenance, the salaries of the staff we hire, the cost of the equipment and supplies necessary to keep these ministries alive and growing.

How much is all this worth?

When reserves were comfortably storehoused, when bank accounts were full, and when cash flowed freely from pew to ministry, we could dance around financial discussions. We could transpose our stewardship responsibilities into donations of time and talent without real impact on our wallets.

But those glory days are long gone. The reserves of the General Assembly are depleted, the cash flow of synod and presbytery have dried to a trickle. And what about your congregation? Can your reserves hold out much longer?

Haggai says, "Who is left among you that saw this house in its former glory? How does it look to you now? Is it not in your sight as nothing?" (v. 3).

There are several designated times during our Christian

calendar when we consider renewing our relationship with Christ. We celebrate his coming during our Christian calendar when we consider renewing our relationship with Christ. We celebrate his coming during Advent. We contemplate the sacrifice of his crucifixion during Lent. But it is only during the stewardship season that we demonstrate the renewal of our relationship with Christ with a long-term financial commitment. This is the season of our most serious struggle. This is the season when we commit not only our hearts and our minds, but also our dollars.

Hear now the words of God through Matthew as found in the sixth chapter, verses 19–21: "Do not store up for yourselves treasures on earth, where moth and rust consume and where thieves break in and steal; but store up for yourselves treasures in heaven, where neither moth nor rust consumes and where thieves do not break in and steal. For where your treasure is, there your heart will be also."

Friends, God has given us the talent, the time, the wealth, and the church. To live "thank-you lives" is to build, to expand, to improve, to grow what we have been given. Our reward is more to build, more to expand, and more to grow, to the benefit of God's kingdom.

How much is it worth?

Gracious God,
Be patient with us. We are quick to complain and slow to learn. Let your mercy show through us as we strive to follow your will and, though the cost be great, keep us faithful to our mission. Help us to determine our fair share and join us together as a network of thank-you lives so that we may multiply one another's gifts to the glory of your kingdom, today and tomorrow. Dear Lord, hear our prayer in the name of the Greatest Steward who gave his life that we may be forgiven. Amen.

In Your Own Words

To God Be the Glory

"Your kingdom come.
Your will be done, on earth as it is in heaven."
                                        Matthew 6:10

About the hardest thing for us to do in this day and age is to trust anybody about anything. Today, to trust is to take risks that may jeopardize our safety and our well-being, not to mention our emotional stability.

This is an age when medical personnel with bogus degrees have provided emergency services, when religious leaders have been found to be child molesters, when police freely execute the violence they have vowed to deplore, and when elaborate sales campaigns dupe the most vulnerable out of their life savings.

To suggest that we relinquish control over what can happen may be considered foolhardy, yet we do it every time we repeat the Lord's Prayer.

If it is pleasant to think of good winning over evil, right replacing wrong, and heaven taking over earth, why is it so difficult to accept whatever happens as the only thing that can happen? Why is it so hard for us to give God the problems we cannot solve, the situations we cannot change? Why do we continue to feel that giving our crises to God is giving up?

Loving Abba,
You hold the key to my inner peace. Teach me to trust that it is your
will that will be done. Help me to allow you to shoulder my burdens
and grant me the ability to know Shalom. Amen.

....

"Truly I tell you, if you say to this mountain, 'Be taken up
and thrown into the sea,' and if you do not doubt in your
heart, but believe that what you say will come to pass, it will
be done for you."

Mark 11:23

When Jesus was hungry, he saw a fig tree but there were no
figs on the tree. Jesus became angry and condemned it to grow
no more figs. Later, when Jesus and the disciples passed by the
tree again, it had withered. Peter was amazed and asked how
Jesus had done it. Jesus had a simple explanation—believe.

How many times do we pray for a miracle and immediately
come up with reasons why it won't happen? Could doubt be
causing the road block in our faith?

Perhaps we may doubt that our prayers have any power, or
that prayer in general is something to do when we can't do
anything else. Perhaps we do not feel we are worthy of favors
or blessings. Good things could not happen to us. Perhaps we
want someone else to do our praying. Remember the popular
radio evangelist who asked listeners to put their hands on the
radio so that he could do the praying? Ever wonder if people
believed that?

The fact is we can develop our own close relationship with
God through prayer. We may smile at the gospel song that
says, "I've got a telephone in my bosom and I can call my God
up anytime," but a close relationship with God can enable us
to know that our prayers have been heard and will be answered in God's way and in God's time.

O Holy Spirit,
Hear my prayer. Cleanse me from doubt that I may always believe
in myself, in you, and in all the things we can do together. Amen.

....

"My God, my God, why have you forsaken me?"

Psalm 22:1

There is so much about faith that is mystical by its very nature.
Sometimes there are no rational explanations, only God phenomena. There are only the phenomena of believing in a power
so much greater than oneself that the "hows" of certain things,
even if explained, are beyond one's capability to understand.

The story of the death of Jesus Christ, like the story of his
conception, is surreal. When we read a psalm written long
before the fact of Jesus, we are as awestruck as those who were
standing beneath the cross.

The same words, the very same words—first from the
psalmist and then from Jesus Christ left to die on the cross.
Take a look at Mark 15:34. "At three o'clock Jesus cried out
with a loud voice, *'Eloi, Eloi, lema sabachthani?'* which means,
'My God, my God, why have you forsaken me?'" It would be
less disconcerting if we could explain it away by saying that
Jesus knew the Torah and was simply reciting what he had
committed to memory. But keep reading.

Compare the taunts of those who suggested the psalmist let
God rescue him if he was so favored, to the crowds who
wanted Jesus to prove he was the son of God by saving himself. Then check out the particulars of both deaths. A mouth
so dry that the tongue of the psalmist sticks to his jaws. We
know that Jesus also suffered from extreme thirst, because he
cried out for water and got vinegar. There is also the matter
of being encircled by evildoers who divided the clothes of the
dying man among them and cast lots for their possession.

The similarities between the two stories are more than an eerie coincidence. The psalm can only be a prediction. Look how it ends, "Future generations will be told about the Lord, and proclaim his deliverance to a people yet unborn, saying that he has done it."

One moment and then another reverberate throughout all time— incredible and truly awesome.

Mysterious and wonder-filled God,
I am struck by the infinite dimensions of who you are. I am hum-
bled by your awesome way of tying events together in ways that can-
not be by chance. I am assured that there is nothing better I can do
than entrust my life with you. Amen.

....

". . . let us live honorably as in the day, not in reveling and drunkenness, not in debauchery and licentiousness, not in quarreling and jealousy. Instead, put on the LORD Jesus Christ, and make no provision for the flesh, to gratify its desires."

Romans 13:13–14

Partying every night, drinking or drugging, indulging unrestrained sexual appetites, bar-room fights, violence and jealousy—sounds like a made-for-TV movie. The interesting thing is that fiction has its own system of morality. Regardless of whether Judeo-Christian theology would label it inappropriate, the more we vicariously witness immoral behavior as an audience, the more we begin to accept the unacceptable.

Notice how much of our society is geared to the comfort and pleasure of the flesh. We want to feel good and we'll do anything to get there. From chocolate to stereophonic sound, if something—anything—gives us pleasure, we want more of it. We will do almost anything to free ourselves of pain, whether physical or emotional. We examine our choices in life in terms of how much is in it for us. It is always considered a "treat" to escape our daily responsibilities so we can cater to ourselves.

The fact is that the morality of fiction is fast becoming the morality of real life. What can we do about that? Paul tells the Romans to put on the blanket of the Lord Jesus Christ.

What a wonderful image! We can put on a blanket of Jesus Christ to protect us from the chill of the night's temptations. Suntan oil protects our skin from the dangerous rays of the sun, while we bask in its warmth. Jesus Christ protects us from the harmful effects of overindulgence, while we submerge ourselves in the joy of living.

O Great God,
Thank you for Jesus Christ and thank you for the protection he can give me. Amen.

"Then he began to teach them that the Son of Man must undergo great suffering, and be rejected by the elders, the chief priests, and the scribes, and be killed, and after three days rise again. He said all this quite openly. And Peter took him aside and began to rebuke him. But turning and looking at his disciples, he rebuked Peter and said, 'Get behind me, Satan! For you are setting your mind not on divine things but on human things.'"

Mark 8:31–33

"Don't nobody bring me no bad news!" The words of the wicked queen from the play *The Wiz* are easy to appreciate. Who wants to hear that things will go wrong? Who wants to hear that someone we know has a terminal illness? Who wants to hear about a child whose life is destroyed by substance abuse? Who wants to hear about homicides, suicides, or genocides? Who looks forward to the unpleasant?

Peter's rebuke of Jesus may well have stemmed from the

premise that people would much rather be uplifted and happy than depressed with gloom and doom. The Evangelism Committee knows that potential new members would not be attracted to the church by accounts of building repair needs, budget deficits, or not enough teachers in the Sunday school.

As a member of Jesus' evangelism team, Peter's motivation may have come from a similar rationale. He may simply have been trying to persuade Jesus to spare folks the gory details and emphasize the positive.

But Jesus was livid. He even called Peter "Satan." Why?

As human beings, things happen to us that we consider good or bad, pleasant or unpleasant, fair or unfair. Opposites create the balance that defines our existence for us. We need one to identify the other.

But could it be that this understanding can only be applied to our lives as they are in progress? We cannot assume to understand the events of our earthly lives as God does. Nor can we judge God's plan for us as good or bad, lucky or unlucky, until we come to the end of the final chapter. Until the whole blueprint is open before us, we cannot attempt to understand the specific "why" of our own existence. For even in death, our lives can take on new meaning for those we leave behind.

O Wise and Just God,
Help me resist any doubt that your plan for my life is a good one.
Help me to be patient when events appear to be unfair. Help me
through my struggle to determine your will and accept it. Amen.

....

"No longer shall they teach one another, or say to each other, 'Know the LORD,' for they shall all know me, from the least of them to the greatest, says the LORD; for I will forgive their iniquity, and remember their sin no more."

Jeremiah 31:34

Jesus came so that we would know God. He died so that our wickedness and injustices would be forgiven. Now knowledge, wisdom, and faith can be ours.

We do not have to be told there is God; we have experienced Jesus. We do not have to depend on the authority or privilege of others to find truth; we have come to understand the Holy Spirit.

Because we are all equal in the knowledge of God, there are none who can say they are better than others because of their family's social standing, the amount of their paychecks, the string of degrees behind their names, or the lack of pigmentation in their skin.

We must only believe in God's mercy to know that we are all good and valuable to him.

O Merciful One,
Thank you for sending Jesus to show me how worthwhile I am.
Help me to trust that I am equal to others in your sight and that my
friendship with my brother Jesus will forgive my mistakes. Amen.

"What then? Should we sin because we are not under law but under grace? By no means! . . . For the wages of sin is death, but the free gift of God is eternal life in Christ Jesus our LORD."

Romans 6:15, 23.

Now here's a question we've heard before. "If Jesus died to forgive our sins, why can't we do whatever we want? Aren't we already covered?" We wonder how many folks do whatever they want to do because they know they can just go to confession, whisper whatever penance is suggested by the priest, and have their "heavenly records" clean from sin.

Who's kidding whom? We know we have not truly given our lives to Christ if we deliberately plan to disobey God's commandments. We also know that if we make a mistake, if we slip and fall, God will pick us up and put us on the right track.

"The wages of sin is death . . ." Paul assures us that we will pay dearly for deliberately immoral behavior, but eternal life is free for the asking. Who can resist a bargain like that?

Dear God,
I know that Christ was crucified for my sins. Keep me ever mindful of that I cannot take advantage of his death and still enjoy eternal life. Amen.

"Alas for you who desire the day of the LORD!
Why do you want the day of the LORD?
It is darkness, not light;
as if someone fled from a lion,
and was met by a bear . . .
But let justice roll down like waters,
and righteousness like an
ever-flowing stream."
                              Amos 5:18–19a, 24

Actually, we've had it pretty easy as Christians in the good ol' U.S. of A. There have been some differences of opinion that have separated us Christians into denominations, but no one has ever challenged the legality of our religion. No one has ever forced us to practice our faith in secret, or fed us to the lions because of it. Consequently, we are not champions of Christianity—there doesn't seem to be a need.

As a matter of fact, we're doing just fine. We diehard churchgoers are there on Sunday mornings—most of the time. But the fact is that if it weren't for our Christian holidays, week-after-week churchgoing could get very routine, even boring, and perhaps meaningless. (Take a look at the descending church membership numbers nationwide!) With Christmas and Easter come the music, feasts, and ceremonies of celebration. We like that. We pay homage to the birth and resurrection of Jesus Christ and call Him "Lord."

But Amos calls this a bunch of hogwash. He's not going to buy it for one minute. "I will not listen to the melody of your harps. But let justice roll down like waters . . ." Ever think about the fact that what is "just" is "deserved" and "merited" as well as "correct," "proper," and "fair"?

To live our faith in true partnership with Christ would leave us vulnerable to the pain of thankless service, the discomfort of sacrifice, and the "foolishness" of forgiveness. Are we sure we want "the day of the Lord"?

Gracious God,
Help us to remain focused on what you would have us do and how you would have the world to be. Separate our loyalties from ritual to fair and just. Return our purpose to be Christians no matter what. Guide us in the way of your son, Jesus. Amen.

In Your Own Words

PART II.

What's the Church Coming To?
Congregation and Denomination

Speaking the Truth in Love*

Genesis 28:10–17 and Ephesians 4:1–16

In the matriarchal culture of African American history, it was the woman's responsibility to be "in charge" as well as to care for her charges. Her role was to love, to discipline, to push, to comfort, to praise, and to insist. She asked for little, but she expected much.

It is with that spirit that I come to you as the new presiding officer of a governing body standing at the door of crisis. It is with that sense of love and responsibility that I speak to you of what I perceive to be the truth in the midst of a collision of collective emotionalism.

I am concerned at what I am hearing—talk of possible secession if the vote regarding the Mt. Auburn Church is not in keeping with one side of the issue or the other. Although the presbytery discussed the ordination of gay and lesbian persons at the request of the membership, the vote is actually concerning Mt. Auburn's proposed noncompliance with definitive guidance from the General Assembly. Apart from the climate of confusion that seems to have been created, what disturbs me most is the possibility that bedroom

*This sermon was preached to the Presbytery of Cincinnati upon my installation as moderator of the presbytery in September 1992. It was at a moment of the controversy in the presbytery over the decision of the Mt. Auburn Presbyterian Church not to comply with the "definitive guidance" policy of the General Assembly of the Presbyterian Church (U.S.A.) regarding the ordination of "self-affirming, practicing" homosexual persons to the offices of the church.

behaviors could in any way determine the fate of our family
of faith.

It is not my purpose to minimize the significance of the issue. It is an issue that generates an intensity of feeling that
cannot be minimized—not if one cares about people as I do.
But it is my role to add perspective. The church does not exist because of the way its structure is administered. Just as a
fire exists because it is burning, the church of Jesus Christ exists because it is doing the mission of God.

In the last few weeks thousands of people were rendered
homeless by a hurricane called Andrew. "Ethnic cleansing"
reduced European nations to the death and destruction of
civil war while hunger destroyed an entire generation in the
African country of Somalia. Why aren't we asking what Christ
would think of that?

Zora Neale Hurston once said, "What I had taken for eternity turned out to be a moment walking in its sleep."

My grandmother's grandmother was a slave in Queen
Anne County on the eastern shore of Maryland. The family
for whom she labored would often travel to Baltimore to worship at a Presbyterian church. And so it was from her seat in
the balcony that my family came to know the empowerment
of education and the privilege of representative government.

Each of us has a faith history and those faith histories have
gathered at this intersection of the here and now to contribute
equally to the totality of our experience.

If you dip a cup into the ocean, your cup will be filled with
the ocean but all of the ocean is not in your cup. And so it is
that each of us can be filled with the spirit of God, but no one
of us is all that God is. In the struggle to determine the will of
God, we Presbyterians do not look to a bishop or a pope to ad-
vise us of that will. We believe the will of God will manifest itself through the will of the body.

Ephesians tells us "there is one body and one Spirit . . . one

Lord, one faith, one baptism, one God and Father of all, who is above all and through all and in all" (4:4).

In *The Once and Future Church* (The Alban Institute, 1991), Loren Mead suggests that "Never before have those in religious congregations had more—potentially—to give to the other structures of society." How exciting to be in this together without the nagging question of whether the leadership is doing what the body really wants to do.

However, with the Mt. Auburn Church question looming over our heads, we have not spent a great deal of energy considering the magnitude of these decisions. We have not thought much about the impact our selections will have on the people in our pews and the region that we serve. Yet, whatever we decide will determine the best use of our dwindling finances and the direction of our mission for years to come.

Because the process of selection presupposes that some things will be chosen and some not, I suspect that there will be those who emerge from these debates with hurt feelings and heavy hearts. Can the presbytery survive further tugs on the already weakened fibers of our sense of community?

Friends, we are living in reality and it is truly an awesome place. The angels in Jacob's dream were ascending and descending on that ladder between heaven and earth. There was continuous motion. There was the tension of opposition. There was constant change—but all were angels of God. We, too, are forced into movement, into dynamic opposition, one way and the other—at the same time and together. Contrary to popular opinion, we are not the "frozen chosen" and we were not baptized in lemon juice! We have a gift for fantastic feelings. Yet the scripture tells us that at the gateway to the kingdom of heaven we must take control of these feelings. We can no longer behave like children—"tossed to and fro and blown about by every wind of doctrine."

We can no longer be children, but we must remain family—

a family of Presbyterians knowing each other clearly and appreciating our differences, a family of Christians capable of living out our faith with passion and emerging in excellence!

"But speaking the truth in love, we must grow up in every way into him who is the head, into Christ, from whom the whole body, joined and knit together by every ligament with which it is equipped . . . promotes the body's growth in building itself up in love" (Eph. 4:15–16).

Jacob's brother wanted him dead—and justifiably so. Crises filled Jacob's life and it was in turmoil that he laid his head down to rest. His dream of the divine showed him the promise of the future, and he awoke with the calm of inner peace and the strength of faith necessary to process the present.

As Jacob awoke from his dream, we shall awaken from this "moment walking in its sleep," knowing that God will never leave us. As my grandmother's grandmother understood, we shall come to understand that God alone holds the answer to the future.

Friends, we are living in reality and it is indeed an awesome place. Yet we will not be afraid for we shall be standing together at the gateway of heaven. We shall discuss, and we shall disagree, but we will always be cushioned with the peace of the Holy Spirit for—"surely, surely—the Lord is in this place!"

Oh God,
You are a gracious and forgiving God.
Holding each of us in the same wise and loving care, help us to
*   focus on you*
so that we can know and understand your will for our lives
*   together and separately.*
Release us from self-love, self-concern, and self-promotion so that
*   we will be able to share*
all that we are, all that we have,
and all that we know in our service to you and to the church that
*   you love.*

We ask these things
in the name of your son, Jesus the Christ,
who first shared it all.
Amen.

In Your Own Words

Home, Sweet Home

Jeremiah 31:7–14 and Philippians 3:12–4:1

The title for this sermon was inspired by a poem by John Howard Payne, in which he talks of "home . . . sweet home" and echoes the sentiment of many when he declares that "there's no place like home!"

Coming home is always a special event. It is an exciting time of anticipated return, of reunion, and of rejuvenation. On the high school or college campus it is a time marked with football, parades, loyalty songs, festive decorations, and all-school parties. Minus the football, we are celebrating the return of friends and family in much the same way. But what is "home"? And what does it mean to come back?

After the death of my mother and then my father, it took me almost two years to bring myself to sell their home in Baltimore. It was simply an empty brick and frame structure. No one lived in it. My son Erik had stayed there while working in Baltimore, but he had changed jobs and returned to Cincinnati. Nevertheless, it was too painful for me to let go.

For me, the house was still filled with sound bytes and flashing icons that triggered my memory when I turned on a light or walked down the stairs. Was I afraid that those snapshots of my mind—along with the memory of my parents—would be gone forever when I sold that house? I had never lived in that particular house, but selling it would mean that I could never go "home" to Baltimore again.

Does that mean "home" is simply a collection of past memories for the purpose of one's sense of identity? If that were the case, if "home" only referred to something that once was, it would be impossible to ever return. Pleasant though one's youth may or may not have been, existing only in the past would make it impossible to live in the present or move into the future.

A poet once said that you cannot step into the same stream twice. Life is dynamic, constantly changing. The streams of yesterday and today flow all too quickly into the waters of tomorrow.

We may whine about the passage of time—especially when we see its effects in the mirror, but there is still something about "home" that we long to stay for regardless of our age. "Home," a sweet and good home, is so important for children to feel safe and to experience love. For adults, it is the sense of the familiar and the comfortable that we crave. It is the security of belonging, no matter where we have been or what we have done.

If you recall the theme song for the TV sitcom *Cheers*, you will remember that it speaks of how we all want to be where troubles are the same, where people are glad we came, and "where everybody knows your name."

Too bad they were talking about a bar rather than a church; but either way, it is easy to identify with the feelings of alienation, isolation, and anonymity so prevalent in today's world. Alienation, isolation, and anonymity were also no strangers to the people of Jeremiah's time.

Judah was caught in the crossfire of Babylon to the north and Egypt to the south. In 587 B.C., Nebuchadnezzar of Babylon broke into Jerusalem, destroyed the city, and took the people captive into exile.

Now it wasn't like they hadn't been warned of catastrophe after catastrophe. You see, Jeremiah started at a young age.

He was born in the suburbs of Jerusalem and his family were priests. So he was called to be a prophet somewhere between fifteen and twenty years of age. For forty years and five kings, Jeremiah warned the people to come back to God, but they didn't listen. After all, he was just the local preacher's kid.

Then, just as it looked like it was all over for the people of Israel, just when it felt like the darkest hour was wrapped around them, Jeremiah came up with a message of hope for a change. God promised them a future.

Jeremiah (31:7–14) describes the Israelites returning home with great joy. They would be gathered together from all over the known world. It would be so great to come home that they would feel like a watered garden. Isn't that the way we all would like to feel? Nurtured and well cared for? They would dance, celebrate, and revel in God's goodness. They could not return to the home they left because they had changed and their "home" had changed. But, they would still be together again, welcomed by God. Home and safe at last.

Today, the church is caught in the crossfire of the rapid changes of the postmodern, information age.

Consider this: People born prior to 1945 are referred to as GI and Depression babies. These folks are adept and quite comfortable with sitting through sermons that go on for twenty to thirty minutes. However, the Baby Boomer generation, born from 1946 to 1965, grew up with television. They are used to programming which is divided into eight- to ten-minute segments separated by commercials.

In addition to selling products, commercials allow time for wandering minds or contemplation of what has just occurred, or perhaps some speculation about what will come next. Needless to say, the Boomer way of information processing will not work for sermons. You let your mind wander for a couple of minutes and good luck getting back into it!

Now when you try to combine Boomers and GI/Depression

Babies with the people born after 1965, you've got yourself a major dilemma. The younger folks came along with the even shorter sound bytes of *Sesame Street* and MTV, not to mention computers! Instant access to instant answers—how can a church service compete with that? It can't, at least not in the traditional sense.

The Jeremiahs of the twenty-first century have warned mainline denominations again and again that emerging generations do not process information in the same way. The news is still good, but the delivery needs adjustment. People of today are into a mindset of self-preservation rather than self-sacrifice. If a person belongs to a church today, it is because that church meets his or her need, not because society says you are supposed to. In the 1950s, one had to be married with 2.5 children, graduate from the right school, and belong to a certain church or denomination in order to get ahead in the corporate world. Now it doesn't make any difference.

We throw open the church doors, say "All right, you all can come in now," and then wonder why the folks aren't lined up two by two. When are we going to look out of our comfort zone to see what really is going on outside? And when are we going to do something about the "ho hum" on the inside that makes people feel like they have to slip out the back? Is the window of opportunity already closed?

Deep down inside, we have to admit that we have noticed the changes in the world around us. We know that families are breaking up and half of our children are being raised by one parent or in "blended" stepfamilies. We have seen how advancing technologies have affected employment trends and possibilities. We know how downsizing has given new meaning to the term "midlife crisis."

Yet, when we think about it, these are the very reasons why church is still a good idea, why church can be our "safe place." Even though the notion of relationship and community may be counter-cultural in the "me-ism" of today, can there really be a substitute for the support of people who care? Is there anything that can compete with the belonging and acceptance in the unconditional love of Jesus Christ? Then why are we keeping it all to ourselves? Why aren't we telling the world that we have the answer? Could it be that we're not speaking the same language? Or maybe we're not speaking at all.

There are a lot of reasons why people move on to some other congregation or drop out of going to church altogether. We have touched on only a few of them. One evangelism resource I read listed thirty-three. However, the "straw that broke the camel's back," so to speak, is indeed not one straw, but many collected over a period of time.

A number of reasons have to do with personal lives or societal situations, but many have to do with the specifics of a particular church. When people become inactive for no apparent reason you can be assured that something isn't right with them and the congregation, or with them and certain individuals in the congregation. People who have suddenly stopped showing up are coming to a slow boil that is bound to spill over onto the inactive members' list and possibly drop off the rolls altogether.

Now if we were to notice a pot of food boiling over on the stove, we would no more stand around and pretend everything is under control than lose a child at Disney World and say, "Oh well, we still have one at home."

The same needs to be true in our church family. We are close enough to hear the rumblings. We can tell when somebody hasn't been around for a couple of weeks. That's the time to ask about what's going on—not six months later or when we need to search for a new pastor. Let's make a promise right here and now that we are going to keep track of each other and that it is okay for the church family to keep tabs on us. Let's contract not to feel like we are prying, but that we are simply caring.

The bad news is that church dropouts are the most difficult people to reach. Their needs are so great and their hurts are so deep.

If we take a moment to put ourselves in the place of dropouts we can recognize how difficult it is for folks to come back, even when the reason for leaving has been resolved. We can sense how things may feel very familiar and yet, somehow strange. We can understand the fear of embarrassment. We can imagine how much dread surrounds too many questions. Returnees want to be recognized, but not bombarded. That's okay, because all we want to do is let them know how good it is to see each one of them and maybe give them a big hug.

The people in the church at Philippi were also a proud people. They were citizens of Rome who liked to do things "decently and in order." They were always striving for perfection and just like us they did not take well to criticism even when it came from within the church.

Paul's letter to them is well seasoned with the joy and deep sense of fellowship that can exist in groups of friends, in congregations, in community. He cautions his friends not to worry about the past because mistakes happen. What is more important is to keep moving into the future and to focus on what is really important—Jesus Christ.

For some there will be distractions along the way: Working two jobs may mean Sunday is the only day to sleep in. Getting older can translate into not being physically able to get around the way we used to. A husband may decide not to keep the kids while the wife goes to church events. Golf partners can only play on Sunday; and so on and so on.

Paul's advice is to "Pay attention to those who follow the right example," because some folks can't or won't. Along with the Philippians, he directs us to rely only on the essence of our faith—the grace of God. And how should we understand God's grace?

In his book *Wishful Thinking: A Theological ABC*, Frederick Buechner paints the picture of "grace" as something we are given like "the taste of raspberries and cream." We experience it in restful sleep, and are surprised by it in our dreams. Grace is realizing that we "might never have been," but that life would be incomplete without us. It is also knowing deeply that whether good or terrible things happen—and they both do happen—God is with us. God loves each one of us, not because of who we are, but because of who God is. We experience grace, joy, and peace because we belong to God. Home is God. Welcome home. Home, sweet home.

O Gracious and Loving Creator,
You bless us with the love of a mother and a father no matter what we do. You nurture us like well-tended gardens and keep us secure. When we entrust our greatest fears to you, you provide us with peace and hope.

You give us the bread and the breath of life, then shower us with warmth from the sun and light from the stars. You have given us "home."

Stay by our side when we walk through temptation this week. Remind us that we belong only to you.

And thank you, Lord, for the privilege of greeting those who have come to be with us this day. We ask that we will find a way to guide many others to the fullness of a life of faith.

We are honored to be your chosen ones and we will serve you wherever and whenever you call on us to do your will. In the name of the one who is our brother by the shedding of his own blood. Amen.

In Your Own Words

MEDITATIONS

Faith, Fear and Difference

"We do not see our emblems; there is no longer any prophet,
and there is no one among us who knows how long."

Psalm 74:9

Okay, here's the thing. Our denomination (the Presbyterian Church (U.S.A.)) is still way over two million members, but
the numbers are slipping so rapidly that we have no idea how
we are going to continue financial support for our ministry
here and abroad.

And who are the prophets of Presbyterianism? Where are the
cheerleaders for our brand of Christian witness? And further,
who can predict how long this downslide will continue? Are
Presbyterians on the road to extinction? We've got ourselves a
problem—a problem that is so entangled in the priorities of our
world that it is almost too mammoth for us to get a handle on it.

So what have we done? We have found other things that
don't matter nearly as much to use up our energies—
church politics and personality clashes. We have shifted our
emphasis away from the things that make us unique—the
way we empower ourselves to govern or the importance of
knowledge for everyone. We have shifted from these things
so that we can concentrate on making ourselves universal
and all-encompassing. We have stretched our theology and the
principles of our faith as though they were rubber bands that
needed to fit around all of last year's newspapers.

50

How long will it take for us to realize what it means to be a Presbyterian rather than a Congregationalist or an Episcopalian? How long will it take for us to decide to showcase our specific style of Christianity? And if the difference in our type of witness is no longer significant enough for us to maintain a separate denomination, how long will it take for us to accept our demise as the will of God?

> *O Great and Powerful God,*
> *Help me to be a voice that others will hear.*
> *Give me the vision to know and the words to persuade.*
> *Give me the heart to embrace what is pure*
> *and the understanding to make it relevant. Amen.*

"There is one lawgiver and judge who is able to save and to destroy. So who, then, are you to judge your neighbor?"

James 4:12

We all have opinions, and in situations that involve planning and decision making those opinions can be helpful. However, when our opinions become judgmental and punitive their helpfulness takes a nose dive.

There is one ultimate law—God's. There is one irrefutable judge—God. How, then, can we begin to assume that we know better or that we can pronounce someone else a sinner?

We know when we are wrong, and when we feel guilty, we ask for God's forgiveness. But who are we to decide that someone else's behavior is sinful? Who are we to decide that their "sinful" behavior—which has no harmful bearing on us—should be punished? Judgment of their behavior is between them and God. If they have truly been in conversation with God and do not feel they have sinned, it is not our place to insist otherwise or to withdraw their rights as human beings. God alone is able to save and destroy.

Blessed Jesus,
I know that you died so that my sins could be forgiven. You also died
for my neighbor so that my neighbor's sins could be forgiven. Keep
me aware that I don't need to judge my neighbor—you will. Amen.

"He came a third time and said to them, 'Are you still sleeping and taking your rest? Enough! The hour has come; the
Son of Man is betrayed into the hands of sinners.'"

Mark 14:41

The scene is the garden of Gethsemane. Three times Jesus
separates himself from his disciples to wrestle with his destiny.
It is hard for him to accept the will of God and he returns to
his friends for support and understanding. Emotionally
strained and physically drained, he seeks comfort from them,
but each time he comes back, they are asleep.

Are we asleep when Christ looks to us? Are we doing the job
he expects of us? Or are we daydreaming about the glory days
to come? Have we been lulled into a false sense of security
while secular society continues to gnaw at the very fiber of our
faith?

The growth of Christianity is most prevalent in Africa and
Korea, places where going to church demands more of its
membership than getting up on time to donate an hour of one
day a week to worship. In Communist countries where freedom of religion has not been a given, believers managed to
maintain their faith.

Has Christianity come too easy for us? Is it possible that we
won't miss the water of salvation until the well of convenience
runs dry? Is Jesus giving us a wake-up call? Will he soon be
betrayed again? Has the hour come?

Gracious God,
Wake me up to the reality of the church's fate. Put me on guard to

protect it from scholars who argue their own narcissistic agendas or leaders who yield to temptations of the flesh. Help me to put trust back into the church so Jesus can depend on me. Amen.

"The chief priests and the scribes were looking for a way to put Jesus to death, for they were afraid of the people."

Luke 22:2

Fear is often generated by the unknown. It is the chief motivator of evil. When we fear the unknown, we guard against it by refusing to consider change, by segregating people who are different, by prohibiting ways of life that we do not understand.

The chief priests were no different. They were afraid of the power that Jesus had over the people. They stood a chance of losing their prestige and their control. Judas was also fearful of the power that Christ had. He felt that Jesus was misdirecting people and told them so, but Christ would not listen. So how did Judas and the priests alleviate their fears? They rid themselves of the perpetrator.

Where does this paranoiac fear come from? It still propels evil to annihilate innocence. What makes us think it must be all or nothing? What makes a man harm a woman physically or psychologically when she is no longer interested in a romantic relationship? What prompts him to feel that if he can't have her, no one can?

What drives a person to feel that they must eliminate the competition in order to win? Do fears stem from jealousy or is it just better to be safe than sorry? Must we be so rigid, so afraid, that we close ourselves to the potentials of difference and risk self-destruction?

We sometimes pride ourselves on being different. We say that our differences unite us, but look at our dwindling rolls.

Many who were once a part of us are no longer. Could this be about our fear of changing to meet the needs of those who are different; not racially but theologically; not economically but politically; not socially but educationally?

Like the chief priests, are we afraid that difference will smother our control and deflate our significance?

Dear God,
Continue to remind me that we are all the same to you, that none of us will be favored in heaven because we will all be privileged. Ground me fast to my faith that I may be comfortable with who I am on earth. Open me to new and different leadership and ways of doing things that I may facilitate your will for my congregation, my denomination, and my world. Amen.

"In the time of King Herod, after Jesus was born in Bethlehem of Judea, wise men from the East came to Jerusalem, asking, 'Where is the child who has been born king of the Jews?'"

Matthew 2:1–2a

Many scholars have wrestled with questions of where these three people come from: Were they really kings? Were there really three, etc.? That is all very interesting, but to me, the most significant issue here is one of scope.

God did not send his son for the exclusive salvation of people of European descent. Nor was Jesus to be strictly a "hometown" hero. The visit of the magi is the first clue that Christ's coming, and the system of faith that results from his coming, is multicultural, multinational, and "multi-socioeconomic."

From the very beginning, diversity was an important dynamic to this religion. It is diversity that helps us to expand our experience as well as define who we are as individuals. Particular things—a language, a way of dressing, food or the way it is eaten when compared to others—is how we understand our uniqueness. Would we ever know that there are men who wear skirts without gender confusion if we had not seen one in a Scottish kilt?

Just as important a dynamic is the notion of universality. Diversity and universality may be opposite directions, but they make up the two-way street on which Christianity lives.

We come to this faith with different ways of doing things, with different styles of living, and with different ways of expressing ourselves. But our needs are the same. We all require love and respect. We all want comfort when we are sick and understanding when we are troubled. Christ responds to these human needs regardless of the particulars of who we are as individuals.

It was for this reason that three people traveled from distant places to bring gifts and pay homage to the newborn king.

Gracious God,
Thank you for bringing Jesus into our lives. Help us carry his message to the lives of those who are like us and those who are not. Amen.

"And the LORD said, 'If I find at Sodom fifty righteous in the city, I will forgive the whole place for their sake.'"
Genesis 18:26

Sometimes we wonder if it's worth it. The whole world would appear to be on its way to self-destruction as rapidly as possible. We struggle to recycle as much as we can to preserve the planet, while others—in the name of progress—continue to eat away at the rainforests and the timberlands. We endure the hassle of having our cars tested for emission excesses, while the air is continually polluted with industrial waste. And what about the medical garbage generated by those who propose to keep us healthy? How often do those dangerous pollutants find their way to our beaches and waterways?

Let's not even talk about the destruction of innocent people by warring nations, warring ethnic groups, and warring parents. Why should we try to channel our anger in positive ways? Why shouldn't we take what we want when we want it? Homicide is already rampant. Arson is a daily occurrence. Robbery is an anticipated byproduct of living in certain cities or certain parts of any city.

Why do we continue to attempt to be faithful followers of Christ? Nobody goes to church. Why should we? The idea of reading the paper or watching TV while propped up in bed on Sunday morning is all too tempting.

Could it be that there is still hope for the world? Could it be that just a few faithful will somehow prevent the annihilation of life on this planet?

Holy Spirit,
You have a tolerance beyond my understanding. Help me to remember your ability to forgive when I am so frustrated I want to give up. Help me to know that living the best life that I can live will keep hope alive. Amen.

In Your Own Words

PART III.

Discovering God in Our Family: Stories of Family with Christmas Meditations

The Most Inspiring Person I Have Known

Exodus 4:10–17 and Luke 18:9–17

Those of you who are familiar with my activities in the "handicapped" community—The Mothers of Special Children, the International Year of Disabled Persons, Kids on the Block Puppets, Stepping Stones Center for the Handicapped, etc.—have figured out that my subject will have something to do with people with disabilities. You are right. It is the fire that burns inside my heart.

Society has always been focused on perfection. Perhaps in the beginning, it was a matter of "survival of the fittest," but today it has become a preoccupation. Success and happiness have been translated to mean holding the top position, driving the most prestigious car, living in the right neighborhood, being the perfect host and hostess. We constantly strive to achieve the standards of perfection dictated by the Madison Avenue commercial. We want to buy the products that will make our skin softer, our teeth whiter, our hair more touchable, our underarms drier. The diet industry is booming with pills, books, exercise equipment, and spas. We want to be perfect. We want to look like those gorgeous, healthy, but "average" Americans in the ads. Ah, but the secret is that even those models don't really look like that! How many women can walk down the street while their hair bounces and blows just enough, but nobody else's does?

Of course no one is perfect. But that lack of perfection has nothing to do with God's view of us or his plan for our lives. A case in point is the truth about Moses that we read in the book of Exodus. We all know that God selected Moses to deliver the Jews out of Egypt, but quiet as it is kept, Moses was handicapped! He had a speech impediment. He stuttered, for goodness sake. In fact, the Bible makes it clear that when God told Moses of his mission, Moses could only complain about his disability. How could he possibly accomplish such a task if he couldn't even talk? Moses was persistent, and according to the story, God became really annoyed, but finally suggested that Moses take along his brother Aaron to do the talking.

Interesting isn't it? How important is this business of perfection anyway? I learned the answer from the most inspiring person I have known. He is only eleven years old, cannot talk or use the toilet by himself, has an IQ of thirty or less, requires constant supervision because of hyperactivity and a seizure disorder—yet, he is one of the most profound teachers of life that I have ever encountered. He helped me plant both of my feet squarely on the ground and turned my priorities completely around. He is my son, Ivan.

Ivan's disabilities were not apparent at birth. His only difference from other babies and toddlers was that he was much better looking. Smooth, clear skin; soft curly hair; and the most incredibly thick eyelashes you can imagine—just as prescribed by the gorgeous baby ads.

He was a busy baby. He could climb, and he could hoist himself over the ends of the crib with the ease and grace of a world-champion pole-vaulter. This actually ceases to be impressive at 2:00 A.M. when one is awakened by the sound of dishes crashing from the sink. It wasn't until he was eighteen months that we decided some further medical advice was in order, particularly in the interest of safety. Our pediatrician directed us to Johns Hopkins Hospital in Baltimore, where we were living at the time. There Ivan was given medication for hyperactivity and subjected to a battery of physical and psychological examinations.

It was at the summation of the results of all these tests that we learned that Ivan was retarded. It was beyond belief! Hyperactive children were usually above average in intelligence. It was a knockout punch that we never saw coming. I cried for seven days and vowed never to set foot outside of my door again. It was in the midst of all this gloom and doom that Ivan began his work.

The first lesson was on the healing power of laughter. I must admit that I was a reluctant student, but Ivan's laughter was spontaneous, uplifting, and contagious. Almost anything could spark it—a favorite toy, a friendly visitor, splashing in the bathtub. Even now, when I go to visit him in Philadelphia, concerned about his care or how far we must travel to see him, I am greeted with peels of laughter. And we laugh together—a joyous, effervescent laughter that makes me feel much better than tablets bubbling in a glass. There are no words spoken, but I hear Ivan saying, "I am a happy person, not an insurmountable problem."

The second lesson was about happiness. What is happiness? It's all relative you say. Yes, it is relative, but it is also self-induced.

We are always looking for things—or people—who will bring us happiness. We want to do all the things that are supposed to make us feel good. We see happy faces swimming, playing tennis, golfing, boating, jogging, so we want to try. But the miracle is not in the sport. Actually, unless we put something of ourselves into the playing of the game, it can quickly become tedious and boring. The same is true for people.

Often the adolescent struggle to be a member of the "in" group carries on throughout life. Many people never learn that the "out" group whose members actually like themselves can become the "in" group. The same is true of collecting material things to gain happiness. Yet the wealthy teen with every material thing he could possibly want commits suicide.

Happiness is self-induced. It is finding pleasure in who you are and what you are doing regardless of how mundane or routine that may appear to be. Happiness is enjoying the simplest of pleasures without worrying about what could be better. I know because Ivan taught me.

He was about four or five and in a program at Stepping Stones, but they were having a semester break. Any parent whose kid is on vacation wants to know the secret of getting their regular chores done while managing to keep the kid happy and occupied. I wasn't even going to try. Besides, I figured, Ivan deserved a nice outing. We both did. For days I had been making mental lists of the possibilities. The library was definitely out. Swimming at the "Y" was out, because they had regular classes scheduled in the pool. The zoo appeared a good prospect even though I dreaded packing up a manageable lunch. (Ivan couldn't handle sandwiches.) Plus, I would need diapers and at least two clothing changes in case of emergencies. I even wondered if Ivan would notice the animals! But, as I said, he deserved a special day.

When the special day arrived, I had managed to get the others out, put a load in the washer, and dress Ivan before the telephone rang. While I answered it, Ivan discovered Vaseline and how well it spreads over one's face, clothes, furniture, and walls. Add a little baby powder and one had a mess that took mother the rest of the morning to clean up.

After lunch—and a hearty dose of laughter—I decided we were having an outing even if we just took a walk. We walked to the empty field by the school at the end of our street. There were no houses, no cars, no crowds of people—just the beauty of God's green earth. I released Ivan's hand. He took a few steps and turned to look at me to be sure it was okay. I smiled in reassurance and he took off running and running in the pure pleasure of it. He fell to roll, letting the soft grass caress his cheek. He laughed in delight as a butterfly swooped down to light briefly in his hair. How simple, yet how special are the things in life that we nonretarded people take for granted!

We talk a lot about freedom in this country and wonder if we really have it. But a great deal of our restriction is of our own doing. We compulsively regulate our lives and often our leisure, but if we were to postpone our schedule to just sit for a minute, we could feel the freedom that Ivan felt. We could feel the same pleasure as a soaring bird or a free-floating balloon. And have you ever really looked at a blossoming flower—really looked? What about a stately tree, or the face of another human being? Then there is the simple pleasure of a song. It costs nothing to sing, but, oh, the pleasure it can bring.

Another one of Ivan's lessons is on the meaning of achievement. We can find satisfaction in our achievements, but how far do we need to go to reach satisfaction. Perhaps we don't need to climb high mountains or circle the world in a hot-air balloon to feel good about what we have achieved. I was impressed with the successful mission of the space shuttle, but I was ecstatic watching Ivan select his toothbrush from the rack, brush his teeth, turn on the water, and fill his glass to rinse his mouth. It was all I could do to restrain myself from hugging him before the process was completed.

The student teacher gazed at us in wonder as he said, "I never thought that brushing your teeth could be such a big thing." But it is, and so are many of the other milestones of personal accomplishment that each of us can reach on an everyday basis. It is indeed phenomenal that we cannot appreciate the miracles of our accomplishments and our capabilities unless there are people like Ivan to put things into the proper perspective. Perhaps that is what Christ meant when he explained to the disciples that the man was not blind because of his sins or those of his parents, but to demonstrate the power of God.

The last and most significant lesson from Ivan is unconditional love. Perhaps because Ivan is unaware of the complications people can add to interpersonal relationships, he has always loved without restraint or restriction. Whenever my relationships with other family members was strained for whatever reason, I could go to Ivan's room. He would always stop his play long enough to give me a warm hug, and I would know that I was still loved and still lovable. This is the unconditional love of Jesus Christ given to each one of us.

This love, pure and spontaneous, is a gift that most of us have to struggle to understand, let alone to give. We have to learn that loving someone does not mean changing them into what we want them to be. Nor does it involve convincing people to think as we do. It is not synonymous with judgment or even with agreement. To love each other despite mistakes made or harsh words delivered is a difficult but priceless gift. As Christians, we must work hard at loving each other as God loves us. We still have to learn to reach out to the "unlovable" and hold each other close despite our differences. To know that someone cares is not only important, it is basic to survival in bad times and prosperity in good times. I miss the frequency of Ivan's hugs now, but the feeling will always be cherished.

I have watched Ivan work his love-magic on others. When my parents had joined us in Philadelphia for Ivan's birthday, everyone else was involved in dinner preparations, so my mother and Ivan were left to occupy each other. Suddenly, Ivan began to jump and clap in double time—one of his favorite things and truly an amazing feat. Then he stopped, took his grandmother's hands, and smiled, inviting her to share his pleasure and jump with him. She took the risk and they jumped and they laughed and they fell into each other's arms. Tears came to my eyes. My mother has had such a difficult time accepting. Now she is telling everyone about the wonderful time she had with Ivan.

I have talked about a lot of things, but I hope you have not missed the main point. Retarded people are not to be feared, or even pitied, for they have been blessed with a lifetime of the purity and innocence of childhood. The experience of knowing and loving a retarded person is to enrich your life beyond measure. There is so much for you to learn.

Great God,
I have delivered your message as it was taught to me by your tiny messenger. I have spoken of the power of laughter, the beauty of living, the gift of loving and being loved. It is done, but Dear Lord, don't let it be over! Let the words of my mouth and the meditations of all our hearts be as pebbles tossed into a clear stream. Let the ripples grow into ocean waves that will slowly, but surely, change the sands of time and with them the old ways of thinking. Bless this congregation as it struggles to celebrate individual difference and help its members to broaden this notion of uniqueness to those with physical, emotional, and mental impairments. Guide us, O God, in the preparation of your kingdom on earth. Amen.

A SPECIAL NOTE:
Ivan passed away unexpectedly in May of 1992 at the age of twenty-two. I know he has gone on ahead to make a way for the rest of us. I wrote the poem on the following page at the time of his death.

After the Goodbye Is Gone

What happens to the souls of special folks like him?
Do they soar up to God like the wings of eagles?
Or do gentle angel hands guide them to heaven
as they were guided here on earth
I THINK THEY SOAR.
What happens to our memories of special folks like him?
Do they fade into the mesmerizing relief
of no more suffering?
Or does the painful space between yesterday and today
continue to gnaw at our consciousness?
Do the tears remind us that we still hurt?
Or do they ease the way from a constant dull ache
to an occasional heavy sigh
EVEN WHEN MY HEAD FINDS COMFORT,
MY SPIRIT BREATHES DEEPLY.
And what happens to the spirits of special folks like him?
Do they collapse—
Exhausted from a lifetime of being different?
Or do they touch the tips of earthly hearts
like a butterfly touches
a field of softly swaying wildflowers?
I THINK THEY TOUCH US—
EVERY NOW AND AGAIN—
WITH THE BITTERSWEET KISS
OF FOREVER AFTER JOY.

In Your Own Words

Surviving the Weeds

Romans 8:15–28 and Matthew 13:24–30, 36–43

When I talked to my mother last weekend, we swapped amazing coincidences. I told her that I sang "Precious Lord" with Karen Stewart and she said, "That's amazing, I was just thinking about that song . . . and you were singing it."

I said, "You want to hear something else really amazing, Jim asked me to preach the sermon for him next Sunday."

"And . . . ," she said.

"And you wouldn't believe the lectionary text (Matthew 13) I'll be using. Talk about apropos . . ."

"What is it?" She asked, and when I told her she said, "Oh . . . do you think you can do it?"

"What do you mean?" I asked. "It's so appropriate; it was meant to be. Of course I can!"

"No, no, no. That isn't what I mean. I mean can you do it— can you stand up there and do it without breaking down?" (This is a very important question to my family.)

"I don't know," I said. "It's not like I'll be standing in front of a bunch of strangers. I mean these people know me. They're my friends. If I break, it'll be okay. They'll wait for me. They'll understand . . ."

"Well, all right," she said.

"Well, all right Mom, this one's for you."

Can we survive the weeds? Why do bad things happen to good people? Living would be so much easier if we didn't

70

always have to struggle for the "right" choices. Can't we just rip out the weeds before they have a chance to take over the field? Do we have to suffer to grow?

My mother lay in a hospital bed at the Johns Hopkins Hospital awaiting her fourth chemotherapy treatment. Between the cancer and its hoped-for cure, her body had been reduced to a memory of what it once was. But her eyes, bright despite the tears, searched mine.

"Do you remember," she asked, "how I always said I wanted to go in an airplane accident? That's the quickest way, you know—nothing long and drawn out. Now here I am, suffering and riddled with pain—just what I didn't want." She covered her eyes and wept openly. "I know it's Thy will and not mine," she whispered.

"We, too, are the children of God—destined to shine like the sun in God's kingdom. But if we are able to share the glory of [Jesus], we must also share his suffering. . . . Yet what we suffer now is nothing compared to the glory He will give us later. . . or we know that even the things of nature, like animals and plants, suffer in sickness and death as they await this great event" (Rom. 8:17b, 18, 22, TLB).

Now there is only the waiting. Last week we received word that the chemotherapy did not work. It is estimated that she has only six more months to live, and we are in the process of getting things in order—organizing finances, researching hospice programs, checking on nursing home facilities for my father as he too approaches the final days, planning the funeral, determining a place for burial, formalizing a will—such are the things you busy yourself with as you cry and you wait.

"If we are hungry, or penniless, or in danger, or threatened with death, has God deserted us? No, for the scriptures tell us that for his sake we must be ready to face death at every moment of the day—we are like sheep awaiting slaughter" (Rom. 8:35a–36, TLB).

Death was never a major shock to my system when I saw it over and over again on television or read about some unfortunate strangers who became automobile accident statistics on a major holiday weekend. Whenever I heard about the death of someone I knew, I suffered sincere pangs of regret and dutifully expressed condolences to the family. When the deceased were more than acquaintances, I struggled with doing the "right" thing and offered my help where possible.

But only in the last six months, when faced with the imminent death of my mother and my father's near-miss, did I feel the powerlessness, the frustration, and the isolation that come from the depths of one's whole being.

Reality is so unreal. My effort to maintain control has turned my insides out. The anxiety is so overwhelming and the search for clarity so consuming that I find myself constantly exhausted and depressed.

My family and friends suggested I pray. But what am I to pray for? My old-school Presbyterianism has taught me that no amount of begging and pleading will change what God has meant to be.

And in the same way—by our faith—the Holy Spirit helps us with our daily problems and our praying. For we don't even know what we should pray for, nor how to pray as we should; but the Holy Spirit prays for us with such feeling that it cannot be expressed in words. And the Father who knows all hearts knows, of course, what the spirit is saying as he pleads for us in harmony with God's one will (Rom. 8:26–27).

Somehow the strength and the energy come, but mostly I have been angry and annoyed and frustrated and feeling guilty. Everybody makes demands of me and nothing I can do is "right" or enough. I have questioned my self-worth. Who am I? What is my purpose? I've got plenty of education, but what am I doing with it? Nothing but finding personal affronts in the behavior of others. It is true. Nothing drives home the meaning and the vulnerability of life better than pending death.

We should not be like cringing, fearful slaves, but we should behave like God's very own children, adopted into the bosom of his family and calling to Him, "Father, Father." For his Holy Spirit speaks to us deep in our hearts, and tells us that we really are God's children (Rom. 8:15–17).

I sought professional help. They told me not to feel guilty, I was doing as much as I could for her. Indeed, nothing more I could do would make everything "all right" again. I could not prevent my mother's death or even take the pain away no matter how hard I tried to find the most conscientious physicians or the perfect nursing care. If my mother chose not to eat, that was her choice, and nothing I could offer would ever be appetizing enough to entice her. The words of the professional offered little comfort, just more reality.

Then miraculously, I wandered into a bookstore—as I often do when in search of diversion—and my attention was drawn to a book by Elizabeth Kubler-Ross called *On Death and Dying*. My pastor had suggested I read it again, but in all the confusion I had forgotten. I purchased the book and took it on the airplane to read on the way to Baltimore.

I buckled my seatbelt, pulled the book out, and it all came back to me—the five stages of grief that helped me years ago to accept my son's brain damage. They were here again, making considerable sense but in a different way. Clarity began to seep through and I read with excitement.

I took the book to the hospital and although I tried to hide it, my mother caught me reading and sensed my awkwardness. Again her eyes searched mine. "Maybe I should read your book," she said with a slight smile.

I jumped at the chance to talk, to dispel the cloud of the unspoken. I told her about the great things I was reading and even read some of the profound passages and inspirational prayers.

And then she talked. She told me about her loneliness, and her disappointment that many of her good friends seemed to be avoiding her. We talked about how people shy away when they don't know what to do or say, how some people still believe the myth that cancer is catching. She admitted being jealous of those her age who were still leading active lives. We talked about ways to make people more comfortable and willing to visit. We talked about the things they could do for her when they asked—reading the paper, writing notes, running errands. We talked about the things that mattered!

And then she told me how much she loved me and appreciated all the things I tried to do. I told her how much it meant to me to hear her say so and our protective shields came down. We cried in each other's arms.

We are saved by trusting. And trusting means looking forward to getting something we don't yet have, for a person who already has something doesn't need to hope and trust that it will be returned. But if we must keep trusting God for something that hasn't happened yet, it teaches us to wait patiently and confidently (Rom. 8:24–25).

Our journey of faith, my mother's and mine, is far from over. We are still learning and growing from each other's strengths and weaknesses. There will be many more weeds and we will continue to stumble in finding our way to that final day of peace and rest.

But what about your journey? How much time and energy have you put into exploring your feelings, beliefs, and fears about the end of your life or those of your loved ones? Suppose like my mother you were told you had a limited time to live? Would it change the way you are presently conducting your life? Are there things you would feel an urgency to do before your time is up? Would there be a need to work out emotional and practical matters with your parents, children, or siblings?

I am sure this is not what you had in mind for a beautiful summer's day, but facing death means facing the ultimate question of the meaning of life. After all, it's not really the dying that is so hard—anybody can do that. What takes skill and understanding is the living of each day as if it were the last.

What, with God's help, can enable us to experience the greatest good our lives can achieve? Here are four suggestions:

1. To develop a sense of personal awareness. Who am I? Now. Here. We should do away with the expected molds of behavior fashioned by our families, our employers, our friends, and our public images to get in touch with the freshness and vitality that come from our original awareness, our own needs, our own choices.

2. To refocus on some of the things we have learned to tune out—noticing the budding of new leaves in the spring, wondering at the beauty of the sun rising each morning and setting each night, taking comfort in the smile or touch of another person, watching a child grow and sharing his or her wonderfully enthusiastic approach to living.

3. To share our newfound awareness with others, especially those who are important to us. Telling another person what is really important to us at the moment is difficult and requires a difficult commitment. The same is true of listening. How many times are we so full of our own thoughts and responses that we fail to listen closely enough to grasp what the other person is attempting to say? But it is through communication that we can enjoy a true sense of belonging to others. We can experience ourselves as full persons only to the degree that we allow ourselves that commitment which keeps us in creative dialogue with others.

4. To determine, with God's help, a unified sense of direction. A personal blueprint, if you will, of what we shall commit ourselves to and how we will go about living that commitment.

Knowing who we are, being aware and appreciative of the world around us, communicating the things that are most important to us, and having a way to live our lives, is being one with our present, whatever it is. It is what makes us truly alive. It is shalom.

For his sake we must be ready to face death at every moment of the day. We are like sheep awaiting slaughter. But despite all this, overwhelming victory is ours through Christ, who loved us enough to die for us. For I am convinced that nothing can ever separate us from his love. Death can't and life can't. The angels won't, and all the powers of hell itself cannot keep God's love away. Our fears for today, our worries about tomorrow, or where we are—high above the sky, or in the deepest ocean—nothing will ever be able to separate us from the love of God demonstrated by our Lord Jesus Christ when he died for us (Rom. 8:36a–39).

Thank you for letting me share.

In Your Own Words

MEDITATIONS

A Homemade Christmas

"The angel said to her, 'Do not be afraid, Mary, for you
have found favor with God. And now, you will conceive in
your womb and bear a son, and you will name him Jesus.'"
Luke 1:30–31

Why wasn't Jesus Christ created without the hassle of birth
or the time lag of childhood? He was the Son of God. Why
didn't he simply descend from the sky or become shaped from
the earth like Adam? Why couldn't he have just "arrived,"
fully matured and ready for action?

Is it possible that God wanted to be in partnership with a
woman so that Jesus would be sensitive to the experience of being human, of knowing a mother's loving discipline, of sensing
a woman's caring concern, and of understanding the importance women give to relationships?

Without Mary's mothering would Jesus have been able to
relate as well to women—to listen, defend and confide in them;
to speak of himself as a mother hen or to compare God to a
woman seeking the lost coin?

And what of Mary's acceptance of the role God was giving
her? Unlike Moses, she never questioned her ability to do
what was being asked—to birth and raise the son of God.

She did not dwell on the effect of this pregnancy on her life
plans or her reputation or the financial and emotional cost involved in raising such a special child. Her only question was

one of logistics—how exactly she was to be impregnated. Once that was explained, she was more than willing to do her part.

Our question becomes whether Mary has been held in reverence throughout the ages because she was the one God chose or because she chose to accept her charge with the honor, trust, and competence that it deserved.

O God,
You ask us to do certain tasks, to assume roles of leadership and we always want to know why. Why were we chosen? Why do we have to do this? Can we do it next year when it would be more convenient? Lord, help us to be more like Mary—ready and willing to do your will whenever you ask. Amen.

"Then an angel of the LORD stood before them, and the glory of the LORD shone around them, and they were terrified."

Luke 2:9

In a day filled with present-giving and eating, most of us are tired from the weeks of preparation, and welcome the "letdown" when the day finally arrives. We sit back, put our feet up and bask in the warmth of the family and friends that gather in our homes or linger in our hearts.

But suppose we didn't know that this was a day to be celebrated? Suppose we had no idea that Jesus Christ would be born on this day? What if we were not aware that he was the Messiah who would one day liberate us from our sins? How would we behave if, suddenly, the glory of the Lord was shining all around us? Would it get our adrenaline pumping or would we consider it some kind of scientific phenomenon to be explained later by experts? What would we do if an angel appeared before us with a message of joy and happiness from God? Would it spark our interest, or would we blame sleep deprivation and look for a place to lie down? And how about a performance by a mass choir to rival the May Festival Chorus and the Mormon Tabernacle Choir combined—would that get our attention, or has loud music become too commonplace in this day and age?

Dear God,
Help us to make today the day that we are as "simple" and uncomplicated as those shepherds with whom you shared the warmth of the Good News. Show us how today can be the day that we feel good about ourselves and become excited all over again—not because of that gift from Aunt Susie, but because of the ultimate gift of Jesus Christ. Amen.

"But just when he had resolved to do this, an angel of the LORD appeared to him in a dream and said, 'Joseph, son of David, do not be afraid to take Mary as your wife, for the child conceived in her is from the Holy Spirit.'"

Matthew 1:20

And what if Joseph had rejected the angel as an illusion resulting from too much caffeine and too little sleep? Mary would have been another statistic—a poor, pregnant, and unmarried teenager.

What kind of options would she have had? Assuming Herod's biggest interests were collecting taxes and retaining rule, we can surmise that the government had not taken away Mary's right to choose among all the possible options. But can we also assume that Mary would not have chosen abortion? There was no chance of her child's having a handicap or a serious medical condition. He had not been conceived in violence. Mary's life was not in danger if she went full term. She was prepared and eager to raise a child.

Jesus was wanted! There would never be resentment, hatred, or mistreatment because he had interrupted educational plans, spoiled employment opportunities, created financial strain, or was simply too difficult to take care of.

As we continue our celebration of new life, let us consider directing our energies to providing a healthy, caring environment for children who have already been born into our world. Let us move away from arguing about decisions that belong to others and concentrate on the welfare of the lives God has already given us, regardless of the circumstances of their conception.

Dear Savior,
Help us to spend this decade campaigning against neglect, against malnourishment, and against child abuse. Let us resolve that each gift of birth will be cherished, nurtured, educated, and protected so that each potential new parent will understand and appreciate the responsibility of creation. Amen.

"Let the sea roar, and all that fills it;
the world and those who live in it.
Let the floods clap their hands;
let the hills sing together for joy
at the presence of the LORD, for he is coming
to judge the earth."
Psalm 98:7–9a

"How beautiful upon the
 mountains
 are the feet of the messenger
who announces peace,
who brings good news,
who announces salvation,
who says to Zion, "Your God reigns."
Isaiah 52:7

Christmas Day

A birth announcement is a way that we share the joyous hope of a new life. The prophets of the Old Testament announced the birth of Christ long before it actually happened. Again and again, they used images of the height of tall mountains or the ends of the earth to describe the impact of this most important birth. They used words like "peace," "joy," "victory," and "glory" to proclaim the anticipated results.

But suppose what the scholars tell us is true—the decline of the mainline Christian churches is partly a result of global and philosophical broadening. Research indicates that the general population of the Western world no longer considers Christianity to be the only system of spirituality and morality, but one of many such systems that define right from wrong, good from evil, life from death.

Does that mean the shouting is over? Not in the least. The good news of salvation is spreading through Korea and Africa faster than the brush fires of Southern California. There is a burning desire to know Christ in places where there have always been other "systems of spirituality and morality."

Why Christianity? Could it be that the same excitement and energy that we experience in the Old Testament have spread to another time and place? Year after year, it is the announcement of the birth of Christ that rejuvenates that excitement and energy for Christians all over the world—churched and unchurched.

Should we stop shouting? Never. The birth of Christ will always be good news for anyone who cares to know what the happiness is all about. HALLELUJAH! CHRIST IS BORN!

In Your Own Words

PART IV

Up Close and Personal with God: Our Personal Relationship with God

The "Yippee!" Factor

Psalm 148 and Galatians 4:4–7

Now that Christmas Day is over, we have time to reflect on what the commotion of the holiday meant in the rhythm of our lives. The celebration of the birth of our LORD and Savior Jesus Christ interrupts the day-to-day routine of ordinary time to bring a joyful anticipation of what is to come. That spiritual joy, that sense of hope, that happiness that makes us sing inside and out is what I refer to as the "yippee!" factor. It is that sensation of feeling good all over that seems to come automatically at Christmastime, even to those people who don't think they are into "God-type things."

The "yippee!" factor invigorates us and sets our hearts to pumping with great enthusiasm. We get excited thinking about what we can do to make other people happy. We immerse ourselves in the pleasure of deciding what gifts will give the most delight to our families or prompt a friend's smile. We think about those that are less fortunate and follow through with good deeds. We donate food for the hungry, buy toys for orphans, distribute coats for the needy, and sing songs to people who are sick or lonely.

December twenty-fifth arrives whether we are ready or not, and it never fails to give us pause to focus on our blessings. We listen to upbeat or sentimental music, light candles all over the house, open presents in a wild frenzy of activity, and eat more than our share of tasty treats. It is a wonderful day for indulging our families and drawing others into the intimate circle of our good feelings. We bask in the glow of love and good cheer until the night comes and snatches the "yippee!" factor away.

December twenty-sixth finds us trying to return to the order and predictability of ordinary time. We are left to marvel at how good we were feeling and how miserable it is to return to life as usual. Well, maybe we don't have to.

No doubt there are many sermons being preached with great suggestions for carrying the spirit of Christmas throughout the year and we're not going to be much different. Let's take a good look at the "yippee!" factor to see if the phenomenon of Christ's birth can splash the rest of our days with the sparkling, sensational, and satisfying color of Christmas Day.

Born of a Woman

Paul's letter to the churches in Galatia begins at the beginning. "But when the fullness of time had come [when God had decided humanity was ready and the time was right], God sent his Son, born of a woman . . ." (Gal. 4:4).

Have you ever wondered why the angels didn't just bring Jesus Christ down from heaven? After all, we are talking about the Son of God here. There could have been a cast of thousands singing great Hallelujah choruses and flashing special laserlike beams all over the earth so that people would be paying attention when the clouds opened up and the angels floated down to earth with this very special child.

For that matter, why did God start Jesus out as a kid? Couldn't he have arrived fully grown? There could have been a giant puff of smoke that was simulcast all over the world. Joining hands across the globe, everybody would have looked up to the sky and Christ would have come flying in on wings like superman—or he could have propelled himself from some giant, golden bungee cord—or he could have simply materialized with tinkling background noises like on *Star Trek*. Cutting right to the chase, he could have saved people from their sins and headed on back to heaven and his rightful place at the right hand of God in less than half the time it actually took.

If you're feeling like this is getting very close to silly, if not blasphemous, you can see that the arrival of Jesus Christ could not be about magic and special effects. Yes, there was something surreal about the star in the East and the wise men following that star, but it was not so far from reality as to be unbelievable. And that is exactly the point.

It was important for Jesus Christ to be born like every other human being because it helps us to relate to him. It allows our familiarity with his experience to enhance our belief that this is someone to be trusted.

Think about it. How chummy could you get with somebody or something that just dropped in from outer space? Would you be able to hear and appreciate the message if you were still hung up on figuring out how this alien type got here, or if you were so frightened that all you wanted to do was run away?

Instead, what we have in Jesus Christ is a fully human being—a being who has proceeded through the appropriate developmental stages of childhood, a being who has experienced the love and discipline of concerned human parents, a being who has lived in a human family with responsibilities for each other, and therefore a being who understands the humanity of our experience.

Now here is something to get excited about! God was so concerned about our ability to relate to his son and his son's ability to model for humanity that he prepared Jesus with thirty-plus years of human aggravation. It is precisely because of that experience that we are assured that Jesus understands our pain, knows our deepest desires, and answers our most perplexing questions as someone who has "been there." God put Jesus through the trials and tribulations of maturing into adulthood just so we could accept him as our brother, just so he could save us from our sins and we would believe. God does indeed love us and that is a fact worth getting excited about at any time of the year.

Born under the Law

Paul's letter goes on, ". . . God sent his Son, born of a woman, born under the law, in order to redeem those who were under the law . . ." (Gal. 4:4b–5a). This needs to be in context so we can understand why Paul was so emphatic at this point.

To start with, the letters of the New Testament are examples of what each of the apostles was teaching new Christians. Together, these letters incorporate what we believe as Christians with guidelines for behavior.

The book of Galatians is Paul's letter to the churches he had started somewhere between his first and second missionary tours. Galatia was a huge province of the Roman Empire that reached almost from coast to coast across the mountains and plains of what is now central Turkey.

Shortly after Paul's visit, those same churches were visited by Jewish teachers who insisted that these Gentiles needed to be circumcised and observe Jewish law before they could be saved. Paul was furious when he wrote to the Galatians. When he was among them, he had taken pains to explain that salvation was not something that could be earned, whether by adhering to Jewish law or some other ritual. The Galatians were to be Christians not Jews. He wanted them to understand that salvation and new life are gifts of the grace of God for all who believe.

The same good news is true for us. We don't need to average a particular number of good deeds per year, nor do we have to subject ourselves to injustice or punishments or hard labor or special cleansing to enter into relationship with God or to find forgiveness for the mistakes we have made. There is nothing to be earned; Jesus has already paid the tab.

But these Jewish teachers must have been so rigid and assertive that not only were the Galatians beginning to doubt what Paul had taught, but also by what authority he taught it. What was written in the ancient books of the scripture appeared to take precedence over the good news of Jesus Christ simply because it was a concept that had been around longer. Plus, there it was, written in black and white, so to speak, and Paul's teachings were strictly word of mouth, yet they pass the test of time.

In essence, the Jewish leaders were saying, "Oh yeah, this salvation business is great stuff, but it's strictly for us Jews. If you Galatians want to get to heaven with us, you're going to have to make Jews out of yourselves." When we consider that Paul's teaching was probably avant-garde for that day and time, we can understand why the Galatians might have become skeptical.

I remember the summer between my junior and senior years of high school. I was traveling across the country with my Uncle Donald, my Aunt Marian, and my cousin Linda. We stopped in Salt Lake City to see the Mormon Tabernacle. I was actually looking forward to the tour. I had an album of the Mormon Tabernacle Choir singing Broadway show tunes and my daydream was to catch them in rehearsal or something. What I got instead was a bucket of ice-cold reality to drown my enthusiasm.

In the first place, anybody who wasn't a Mormon was not going to get into certain buildings and only certain "levels" of Mormons could get into the sanctuary. While I was trying to understand the nuances of angel status and levels of spiritual achievement on earth, my aunt had separated herself from the family and was confronting the tour guide regarding race and acceptance into the Mormon religion. Once I found out that a black person could never enter the tabernacle nor reach anything but the lowest level of angels regardless of what they did, that was it for the Mormons in my book.

It is not hard to imagine that the churches in Galatia were going through some similar misgivings about their new-found religion, especially after the Jewish teachers had finished their little "dog-and-pony" show. Can you blame Paul for blowing his top? He starts ranting and raving in the first chapter and by the third chapter he is calling them "foolish" and "bewitched."

Paul's frustration stems from wanting the Galatians to understand that Jesus Christ was "born under the law"—he was born a Jew subject to the laws of Judaism, which he studied inside and out—just so he could rescue others from the rules and regulations that would block their way to the kingdom of God.

One does not have to be Jewish before they can be Christian and find salvation in Christ. All you have to do is believe. You don't have to be a particular race, gender, or nationality. You don't have to eat certain foods, undergo surgery, study ancient law, or repeat particular prayers. All you have to do is accept Jesus Christ as your Lord and Savior to receive the grace of God's forgiveness.

Actually, we Presbyterians could spend some time with this idea right about now. It has become more and more difficult for us to attract new people to our denomination and I wonder if that is because we are too busy looking for people who are just like us. We have become so focused on rules and regulations that we have forgotten a very basic tenet of our reformed faith. Unlike popular movies and TV shows, Presbyterians do not believe that angels must perform certain acts to receive wings and enter the kingdom of heaven. Unlike Roman Catholics, who must confess their sins to a priest and do penance before they can be forgiven, Presbyterians believe we confess directly to God and are assured of forgiveness through God's grace.

Yet we have been talking about adding stipulations to our constitution that would have people confessing to their congregations or sessions that they are guilty of infidelity in their marriage or have not been chaste in their singleness. They would be required to somehow demonstrate their repentance before they could be ordained as elders, deacons, and ministers of the word and sacrament. Somewhere there should be warning buzzers going off. Presbyterians believe that God alone is Lord of the conscience and that translates into the elimination of the middle man or middle group of men and women. To be Presbyterian is to be in charge of your own behavior under the direction of the Holy Spirit. To be Presbyterian is to pray and meditate with God to determine what you should do in any given situation. To be Presbyterian is to answer to the authority of Jesus Christ using scripture and the confessions as guides through the maze of right and wrong.

Presbyterians must be careful not to become like the Jewish teachers who insisted on enforcing historic rules and traditional practices that applied to a different time and place and are subject to nuances of language that may or may not be translatable.

Am I suggesting that we live without standards? Not at all. It would be impossible to live together in community without agreeing on how that can happen for the benefit and safety of everyone. In fact, as Presbyterians, structure and guidelines are crucial to the way we witness for Jesus Christ. We believe that our way of governing ourselves can lift us from the debilitation of chaos to the efficiency of order. For us, this is the best way to be about the business of God effectively.

But let's be careful that we are about the business of God and not our own agendas. While there can be comfort and stability in the *Book of Order* of the Presbyterian Church (U.S.A.), it is not in and of itself the promise of salvation for which Jesus Christ sacrificed his life. Just like the brain-teaser that requires one to go outside of the box in order to connect all of the dots inside the box with one line, sometimes obeying God requires flexibility and ingenuity rather than strict adherence to stipulations imposed by people. We are free to have a say in the conduct of our own lives while we live in balance with the needs and rights of others.

When the time comes to revise or enforce the constitution of the Presbyterian Church, remember this: God accepted Abraham long before giving his law to Moses. We don't have to earn God's love; it is already ours no matter who we are. That's something to really get excited about.

Adoption as Children

But hold on to your seat. Paul has more good news. God invites us to be up-front and spontaneous like children. He wants to be treated as our "Daddy." In the privacy of our personal prayers we can bring everything and anything to God. We can be excited and tell God how happy we are. We can ask for help in solving the problems that we have not been able to solve all by ourselves. When we are frightened, we can ask "Daddy" to be with us until the darkness passes into light. We can feel God's loving arms surround us when we feel lonely, and know that we are forgiven when we make mistakes. Paul says that because we can enjoy an intimate relationship with God, that proves that we are children of God. And further, if we are children of God we are heirs to all of God's promises.

Perhaps all we need do to perpetuate the "yippee!" factor is to reacquaint ourselves with the curiosity, the innocence, and the spontaneity of our inner child. Maybe it is time to take ourselves a little less seriously. We could even start having fun going to church. We could start enjoying our brand of religion to the point that we would want to recommend it to everybody. Maybe our curiosity could lead us into exploring new things in worship and experiencing a new appreciation for difference.

Now, wouldn't that be something to get excited about!

Dear Baby Jesus,

So small, so fragile, so vulnerable, yet so fresh and so vibrant, be born again and again in our hearts, be born again and again in every congregation of the Presbyterian Church (U.S.A.).

O poor, homeless child of Bethlehem, be born again in our house, be born again in our neighborhoods, be born again in our cities and in our towns.

O precious son of Mary, be born again in our world and bring us peace. Amen and Amen.

(Inspired by the words of Marian Wright Edelman)

In Your Own Words

Leaping for Faith

Judges 4:1–10 and Matthew 25:14–30

According to Hebrews 11:1, faith is "the assurance of things hoped for, the conviction of things not seen." Definitions from the American Heritage Dictionary describe faith from several perspectives. It is "the theological virtue defined as secure belief in God and a trusting acceptance of God's will," "a set of principles or beliefs," "belief that does not rest on logical proof or material evidence," and "loyalty to a person or thing / allegiance."

The *Book of Order* (G–2.0500) of the Presbyterian Church (U.S.A.) says, "In its confessions, the Presbyterian Church (U.S.A.) expresses the faith of the Reformed tradition. Central to the tradition is the affirmation of the majesty, holiness, and providence of God who creates, sustains, rules, and redeems the world in the freedom of sovereign righteousness and love."

By now it should be as clear to you as it was to me. It is not our belief in the good news of Jesus Christ that needs to be revisited, but what we do with it.

Consider the parable of the talents in Matthew 25. Jesus has given us the gift of his good news and we have buried it like a secret treasure to be kept hidden. Now we are in trouble and that is nowhere more evident than in the drastic numerical decline of membership in mainline denominations.

No matter how often we reorganize our denominational structures or create new programs in our congregations, the

Titanic is still going to sink. We are living apart from the bulk of the population and, in their world, the majority consider regular church attendance a bit eccentric at best and "holier than thou" at worst. Before we can determine a response to this dilemma, we have to answer some very basic questions: Why does the ship of mainline Protestantism need to be saved from certain death at the bottom of the ocean? What difference would the death of Presbyterianism make in the planet's scheme of things? Who cares if the doors of this church stay open? Why do we seem to be in a constant state of panic?

In his recent book, *Transforming Congregations for the Future* (The Alban Institute), Loren Mead suggests that society needs the church and the community graces that the church generates. He says, "Society can define itself and set limits, but we all yearn for a community in which we know that we are cared for and valued in ourselves." He then goes on to comment on a list of ten characteristics of the church community that are offered as essential for public life. Building from ten to one in TV's dramatic style, the count goes as follows:

10. People in congregations are given the power to share their leadership talents.
9. Congregations bring hope and persistence to the political table. "In a society of gangs and drugs, congregations witness to a world in which the lamb and the lion can dwell together."
8. Unlike politicians, people in congregations tend to be more mindful of feelings than concerned about saying exactly what they are thinking.
7. People in congregations take personal responsibility for the well-being of others.
6. Society has conditioned people to lock themselves in for safety, but congregations are places where people who feel isolated can interact with others.

5. Religious communities create drama, music, and festivals to celebrate life together, to give as much hype to community as the general public gives to conflict.

4. Resolution of conflict situations in congregations goes beyond just stopping them to ending with reconciliation and forgiveness.

3. Limited resources are not hoarded but shared in congregations where our biblical training changes the fear of "not enough for me" to the joy of giving.

2. The prejudices and stereotypes that foster fear and cripple the order of the secular world can be processed in churches through experience with others including those outside of our own groups.

1. The church is a place where befriending strangers is not only appropriate, it is expected.

In James Angell's book, *How to Spell Presbyterian* (Geneva Press), he describes Presbyterianism as "an attitude about freedom and the people's responsibility for working out the content and expression of their faith." In *Wishful Thinking*, Frederick Buechner talks about faith as a process, a journey without a map, in which you are not sure where you are going but you are going anyway.

So, here we are, Presbyterians ready to embark on a journey into the next century. We have an attitude of faith and reasons for making the trip, but this faith journey doesn't come with a map. Are we ready to leap into the unknown?

There is an African proverb that says, "If you are on the road to nowhere, find another road." Good advice, but suppose the new road does not look very much like the one we are used to walking? Does it mean we have to venture into the territory of our least favorite things—difference and change?

There is something very different about the passage in Judges where we hear about a woman who was a prophet, a judge, and a head of state long before the birth of Jesus. Who would have thought it!

Historically, the book of Judges covers the 200 years or so between the death of Joshua and the rise of Samuel. Chronologically, scholars estimate Deborah's story to have occurred around 1125 B.C. In this time of transition, the tribes of Israel were held together only because of their common beliefs. Throughout the period the nation's loyalty ran in cycles. The people periodically abandoned God for whatever the pagan society was into at the moment.

The tension between Arabs and Jews existed then as it does now. Each time the Israelites strayed from God, they suffered at the hand of the Canaanites until they pleaded to God for help. God would send a deliverer and everything would be fine until that person died. The people were again attracted to misconduct, and the cycle would begin all over again.

The nation was ruled by a succession of twelve judges—one of whom was Deborah. She held court under a particular palm tree and her primary responsibility was to render legal decisions, but she was also a prophet and led a military expedition. It was in her capacity as a prophet that she summoned Bakar. The Canaanites had been agitating the Israelites in the north but they were afraid to do anything about it because Sisera's army was large and they had fancy equipment like iron chariots. Through Deborah, God was directing Bakar to march against Sisera.

The significance for us today is that Bakar's reluctance to go without Deborah's assistance presented a new paradigm, a kind of "what's wrong with this picture" incident. The situation was so out of the ordinary that Deborah felt compelled to call attention to it. She agreed to go with Bakar, but reminded him that the battle would not give him, the man, credit for victory. The Canaanites would surrender to a woman. Deborah wanted to be certain he was okay with that before she went trudging off with him.

We have seen world leaders who are women—Golda Meir, Margaret Thatcher, Indira Gandhi. But even we would be hard pressed to imagine a woman taking command of the Persian Gulf War or the invasion of Vietnam! How many of us would agree to Deborah's terms in an age where drill sergeants control female recruits with sexual assaults and death threats?

Things turned out okay for Deborah and Bakar; Sisera's army was wiped out in spite of their large numbers and iron chariots. Sisera himself was killed by another woman, Jael, who turned out to be a spy for Deborah.

But let us not forget the point. Victory came when it was not "business as usual." As truth would have it, we have been steering the church with our eyes glued to the rearview mirror of the way we have always done it. "Change and difference" may be uncomfortable for a lot of people, but somebody and something has to help this church of ours survive and move on to the next millennium.

Loren Mead suggests four areas that need our attention:

> the congregation as community,
> proclamation of good news,
> teaching, and
> the serving role.

I would like to conclude with the notion of the congregation as community, or *koinonia*. Sociology, or how we live in relationships, is my primary area of professional interest. I am trained in social work and I am currently working on a doctorate in a new field of developmental sociology. It was in this connection that I was in Washington, D.C., for a ten-day colloquium as part of a residency requirement for my degree.

Twenty students and two faculty conveners gathered. Nobody knew anybody else when we arrived at that table. We came from different cities. We ranged in age from twenty-six to seventy-eight. We varied in economic status, in race and nationality, in life experiences, in gender, in family status, and even in our command of the English language.

Without a handbook of pretested guidelines or the knowledge of exactly what we would have to accomplish or even how long it would take us, it was necessary to establish the perimeters within which we could all work. It was painful. It was uncomfortable. Difficulty turned into disaster. There were major issues of control. At least in congregations, there is a *Book of Order* and enough knowledge of personalities to avoid many of these pitfalls.

Yet, we did come together. We were a model of *koininia* that should be available in congregations, but often is not. Each of us found a personal value and affirmation which allowed us to share some of the most intimate aspects of our lives as well as our academic and professional goals. By the end of that ten days, everyone had laid their hearts bare, even though this was neither required nor listed on an agenda for the day.

Koinonia is trusting that what is shared will find understanding, acceptance, support, and help if requested. How can we get that to happen in congregations? Perhaps, one very simple answer is to provide people the opportunity to share their faith journeys, to tell each other who they are and how they have come to be the people they are. Of course, small congregations have an advantage, but there still needs to be the opportunity for everyone to have a turn in the spotlight and be encouraged to share.

We have come to another one of those leaps of faith. It is amazing to learn that so many "ordinary" people have *extra*ordinary spiritual experiences but do not connect them with their churches. Either they don't think people will be interested, or they are afraid others will not understand. Not only does this make no sense; it is a crucial factor in why fundamental and evangelical churches are growing.

There are so many clues in the secular society that folks are really hungry for spiritual experiences. The number of daily "meditation" calendars seems to have grown tenfold. Popular music wants to know what we would do if God was watching. The candle business is booming. Recordings of chanting monks are among the bestsellers. The Methodist Emmaus Walk retreat has a three-year waiting list. Popular family-time television actually has angels sent from God who dramatize or relate principles of Christian faith.

You don't have to be a rocket scientist to conclude that people—even the unchurched and never-been-churched—are seeking ways to connect with their souls. Why are we mainline Protestants still preoccupied with programs and activities? What was good in the fifties and sixties may not be the best thing for the year 2000.

Koinonia and *community* come from the same Greek root as *communion*. It is in community that we receive the elements that symbolize the body of Jesus Christ that was sacrificed for our sins—all of us and each of us. It is in coming to the Table of our Lord that we become "blood" brothers and sisters with Christ and each other. Maybe once we recognize how we are related to each other, we can begin to be relatives to each other at the gut level. It's important that we get to that point, and it is crucial that we get there soon!

Gracious and Loving God,
We come to you this morning seeking forgiveness. We have separated our personal relationship with you from our experience of being together in your church. Help us rid ourselves of embarrassment and discomfort as we seek new levels of relationship with each other through you.

Lord, we want very much to be the church that our brother Jesus Christ wanted us to be. Send us leaping to that place of fulfillment where you would have us grow in faith and prosper in trust. Teach us to do your will. We ask these things in the name of Jesus, the Christ. Amen.

In Your Own Words

Me and My Abba

"But who can endure the day of his coming, and who can stand when he appears? For he is like a refiner's fire and like fullers' soap;"

Malachi 3:2

Many have been known to approach laundry days with a considerable amount of dread. With the stubbornness of stains, dirty clothes can be reminders of each day's mistakes. But like the ad says, there is a certain satisfaction in knowing your whole wash is clean.

Which wonder detergent will remove the rings of worry from our collars? What super suds will remove the pungent odor of day-to-day drudgery?

Malachi says one will come who can bleach the dirtiest of garments! He will refine and purify our hearts. He will cleanse our souls.

Dear God,

Help us to allow Christ to come into our lives now as we anticipate the celebration of his birth and throughout the year.

Help us to unburden our "dirty linen" so that we may be clean again, worthy to do your work. Amen.

"Be gracious to me, O LORD, for I am in distress; . . . I am
the scorn of all my adversaries, a horror to my neighbors,
an object of dread to my acquaintances; those who see me
in the street flee from me."

Psalm 31:9, 11

It is so hard to stand up for what is right when those around
you disagree. Act on your convictions, take a stand, particularly one that is unpopular, and you will indeed suffer the
consequences—physically as well as emotionally.

Years ago, as a high school student, I turned in the name
of another student I had seen cheating on an exam. The
exam ended with an honor pledge that not only required
students sign if they had "neither given nor received answers," but also that they had not seen other students give or
receive answers.

A number of people had witnessed the cheating, but only
two said so before signing the pledge. Before long, the word
was out on the two that "ratted" on their fellow student. The
toll was the painful emotional pressure of ostracism at an age
when peer approval is critical.

Now students are expected to inform on the kids that take
and deal illegal drugs in an environment of their widespread
use. The pressure is no longer limited to emotional separation. Now we are talking about physical danger.

A known "reporter" risks severe beating and/or death. People have seen women raped, children abused, and senior citizens beaten to death without doing a thing about it. Why? Not
because they think that crime is okay, but because the personal risk is too great.

It is great. But what is our responsibility as people of God?
We have been entrusted with this world and we are the only
ones who can take responsibility for what goes on in it. Yes we
endanger ourselves, but we have to do what we have to do. If

it is not right at school, in the workplace, or around the church, we have to make it right. And God will be with us.

Dear God,

We have names for the symptoms of the psalmist—severe depression, paranoia, conversion reaction—and I know them well. I know the risks. Help me look beyond that to the greater good. I know that I will be in your care, whatever you decide that care to be. Now bless me with the courage to do your will. Amen.

"You desire truth in the inward being; therefore teach me wisdom in my secret heart."

Psalm 51:6

How many times do you do something—subtle, but unfair—that puts you or someone close to you in a more advantageous position? And how many times have you been tempted not to correct a cashier's mistake that was in your favor? Or what about the times you have envied what someone else has or admired someone else's spouse? How many times have you been angry with God for the circumstances of your life over which you have no control?

Hopefully, not as many times as the rest of us, but the laws of probability put all of us church folk in the same place. It's hard to be "holier than thou" when the thou is you. Way down in the heart of who we really are is that nagging knowledge that we have done something wrong today, yesterday, and the day before that. The fact is that if it were not for our love of God, we could get away with it because nobody else even suspects.

But we love God, and our heart of hearts is laden with major guilt. That makes us angry and jealous in and of itself. After all, there are a lot of folks out there that get away with a lot worse—from murder to embezzlement to adultery. All we did was accept something that was not ours. All we did was use a friend of a friend to position ourselves at the top of the list for an appointment or promotion or special favor.

When we realize that we are really angry with God, whom we would prefer to please, we start trying to make up like children caught with their hands in the cookie jar. But God is not into game playing. Whether we deserve it or not, whether we go through a ritual of repentance and sacrificing or not, God will forgive us. Wow!

Gracious God,
I have messed up so many times it isn't funny. Then I make promises to you that I wind up not keeping. But you continue to forgive me, faster than I can forgive myself. Teach me how to be honest with you and myself, in the name of Christ, who died so that my sins would be forgiven. Amen.

"Teach me your way,
O LORD, and lead me on a level path because of my enemies."
Psalm 27:11

When we are facing serious danger, there is no one and no thing that can protect us the way God has and will. We are simply required to ask for God's help and pay attention for the answer without allowing the solutions we have imagined to distract or impair our vision.

Remember the story of the man who climbed up on his roof during a major flood? He prayed for God to save him. When a boat with a rescue team came by he shooed them away saying their boat could turn over in the raging waters. He insisted that God would rescue him. When the water rose so high that the man was sitting on top of his chimney, a helicopter hovered over him. But he refused to grab onto the lowered ladder because he was afraid to fly and knew that God would provide a "safer" way. When the inevitable happened and the man drowned, he supposedly complained to St. Peter that he had prayed for God's help, but God had not saved him. According to the story, Peter looked over his glasses and said, "Well, God sent the boat and the helicopter . . ." We can all imagine what that man was expecting—"Super Angel" or maybe even "all the company of heaven." It is important to trust that God will be there for us—as that man on the roof did. But it is also important to listen for the answer, for the ways we can participate in our own rescue, for God's solution rather than our own.

When a situation is dangerous—a spouse or partner is abusive, an addictive habit threatens our health, the place where we live or work is structurally unsound—it is to distort faith not to do the obvious. And when the obvious is clouded by what is familiar and therefore comfortable, we have to take a risk to make a change. But if we are not willing to take that risk, we are shutting off God's help. God is good to us when we're opened to God's possibilities rather than our own unrealistic solutions.

Blessed Lord,
Why do I always think I know all the answers? Why do I ask for your help and ignore your answer? Teach me your way. Show me how I can see truth more clearly, how I can hear the words that will save me and help me to trust the strength of your power that is always there for me. Amen.

"Then they came to Jerusalem. And he entered the temple and began to drive out those who were selling and those who were buying in the temple, and he overturned the tables of the money changers and the seats of those who sold doves."
Mark 11:15

Anger is an emotion we don't always understand. We tend to cover up our anger especially when we are among people we don't know very well. Anger embarrasses us. It makes us appear impolite or unpleasant and makes even those who are not involved uncomfortable.

But Jesus was not concerned with the comfort level of the people who were in the temple. He used his anger to demonstrate the intensity of what he felt, to change what had become the acceptable status quo. And indeed, anger can be a most efficient force to effect change. It is the energy of anger that propels protest marches, letters to the editor, political confrontation, and healthy debate. Anger is what moves us to do something about injustice or irrational behavior.

The trick is channeling our anger in positive directions.

We would all agree that shooting people in the work place because you were laid off or killing people on a commuter train because society has given you a bad shake are extreme examples of mentally ill behavior—pure and simple craziness. Yet anger is also misused when the manager blames us for bad sales when the economy is down and we take it out on the folks at home.

Spousal abuse is usually prompted by something outside of the marriage, while child abuse often stems from taking care of children who require an abnormal amount of attention—usually because of some impairment. The people who are abusive don't really want to be that way, but they have no clue as to what to do about the energy of their anger. Experts tell us that the best way to channel unproductive anger is through physical exercise, meditation, and/or separation from a potentially volatile situation. Regardless of how we dispel the energy of anger, we must be careful to channel it appropriately.

Abba,
Sometimes I get so angry, I feel like destroying things or hurting

people. Teach me what to do with my anger so that I may follow in the ways of my brother, Jesus Christ. Amen.

....

"For all that is in the world—the desire of the flesh, the desire of the eyes, the pride in riches—comes not from the Father but from the world."

1 John 2:16

"You're old enough not to let your wants hurt you," is an old expression that parents and grandparents have used when children beg for the impossible or the unnecessary. Often God is saying the same thing to us and we should be old enough to differentiate between what is really important and what is not.

We should be, but sometimes we get so caught up in the lights and glitz of luxury that we spend more than we can afford on risky get-rich-quick schemes or stake our dreams on winning the lottery. We measure success by the size of a paycheck or the number of heads that turn when we walk by. Pleasure and happiness transform themselves into things we can see or feel or taste. Beauty is visible and satisfaction is physical. Yet all this relates only to the world that we live in. What of those things that are not of the world, that are realized outside of the tangible? What of the pleasures that last longer than the latest entertainment trends or food fads? What of the happiness that evolves from our spiritual side and feeds on the joy of everlasting life?

Over the ages there have been people trying to find themselves, looking for that which will fill them and make them complete. We know what can fill us and yet we turn to our faith only after we have explored the other possibilities.

Dear God,
Help me to look to you first. Remind me that I cannot find long-lasting comfort in chocolate cake or eternal happiness in a shopping

spree. Lead me to quiet times with you that will enrich my days and renew my life. Amen.

"Reside in this land as an alien, and I will be with you, and will bless you; for to you and to your descendants I will give all these lands, and I will fulfill the oath that I swore to your father Abraham."

Genesis 26:3

Frequently, we find ourselves in situations where we feel uncomfortable because we are different or less experienced than others—in places where we feel "alien" to those around us. Perhaps we found ourselves as the only female in an all-male office, the only white at an all-black party, or the only young person at an all-adult meeting.

Yet, even though we may be uncomfortable, someone must pave the way in order for those who are like us to benefit tomorrow. Someone must endure the embarrassment or the awkwardness. Someone must risk the pain. Someone must learn the new territory even when they would prefer being somewhere else. This is God's message to Isaac. This is God's message to us.

When we find ourselves in unfamiliar surroundings, with people who speak languages foreign to our ears, with ways of doing things that are not our way, it is not enough to tolerate the situation until we can change it. Difficult though it may be, we have to participate fully in all that life brings to us so that those who follow may also enjoy their lives to the fullest.

Being new to any situation means taking risks, but when we can shed a different light, when we can learn something new, we must seize the day or forever lose the chance to make a difference.

Gracious God,

Forgive my timidity. Give me the courage to bloom where I am planted. Give me the stamina to realize the plan that you have for my life and the lives that will follow mine. Amen.

In Your Own Words

PART V.

When Faith Goes Public:
Issues of Social Concern

This Is My Story

Exodus 23:1–3, 7; Psalm 140:1–2, 4;
Romans 8:18–19; 1 Corinthians 12:12–14;
1 Peter 4:12–13, 17

As we celebrate the birth and life of Martin Luther King, Jr., I would like to share another facet of my life with you that relates to the civil rights struggle as I experienced it. Archibald MacLeish said, "There is only one thing more powerful than learning from experience and that is not learning from experience." I want to share mine so that you too may know.

"You shall not spread a false report. You shall not join hands with the wicked to act as a malicious witness. You shall not follow a majority in wrongdoing; when you bear witness in a lawsuit, you shall not side with the majority so as to pervert justice; nor shall you be partial to the poor in a lawsuit. Keep far from a false charge, and do not kill the innocent and those in the right, for I will not acquit the guilty."

Exodus 23:1–3, 7

On April 29, 1992, a jury found a group of white policemen not guilty of a crime that had been videotaped for all the world to see. The disenfranchised communities of East Los Angeles responded immediately with riots. Anger and frustration turned into burning, violence, and looting. Even more disconcerting to me, however, were the results of an NBC opinion poll that indicated a majority of those surveyed did not understand why the people in L.A. were responding the way they were.

I happened to be at a meeting of the Synod of the Covenant Assembly when the news broke. All I could do was cry as I stood in front of that big screen TV to watch the tragedy unfold. Some who saw me offered comforting hugs and handfuls of tissues, but the facial expressions of my fellow Presbyterians were puzzled. Yes, this was a terrible thing, but why was I so blown away? What did any of this have to do with me?

It started in 1954. The Supreme Court handed down a decision in *Brown vs. the Board of Education of Topeka, Kansas*. This decision directed all boards of education throughout the United States to facilitate the racial integration of public schools.

I grew up in Baltimore, which is south of the Mason-Dixon Line. Segregation had limited my experience of whites to Mr. Sussman, who owned the corner grocery store, and the mailman, whose name I never knew.

I found the discussion about integration very interesting but it had no bearing on my life. I lived in a colored neighborhood (we were "colored" then). My family belonged to a colored Presbyterian church, and I attended a colored elementary school. That is until I graduated from the sixth grade and found myself enrolled at Pimlico Junior High School.

It was all my mother's idea. Pimlico was a brand new school and I was in a transition year. According to her that was perfect. I, on the other hand, did not agree. My friends were all enrolled in PS 181 and I had signed up with them. Junior high was frightening enough without adding a bunch of crazy white people! Look what the folks in Montgomery had to go through just to sit in the front of the bus, for heaven's sake! But my mother had made up her mind. She said the Supreme Court had opened the door and it was up to the colored people to walk through it. I just didn't understand why I had to be the one doing the walking.

Mama kept telling me that Maryland wasn't Alabama or Georgia. She explained how the white folks at the school board in Baltimore had decided to proceed with integration as quietly as possible and had spent more than a year developing a plan. It just so happened that the plan for integration, the opening of Pimlico Junior High, and my graduation from sixth grade came at the same time.

I remember my first day very clearly. It was sunny and brisk. My mother dropped me off at the corner of Park Heights and Northern Parkway. The school was a huge impressive building of pink brick and modern arches. There were walkways, concrete benches, freshly seeded lawns—and white people as far as the eye could see.

My mother shooed me out of the car. My first instinct was to run, but my mother was watching. I found a side entrance but it was locked. Someone behind the door pointed to a sign that was taped to the front. It said "Registration" with an arrow pointing to the main entrance. My mother tapped on the horn and pointed in the same direction. I sighed heavily. I have never been very fond of fear and this was heavy-duty stuff.

When I arrived at the main entrance, I noticed several policemen milling around and my heart leapt to my throat. Why were they here? Was there going to be trouble?

I looked around for my mother, but she had finally pulled away, so I sat down on one of the benches and waited for the crowd to thin out. I watched as friends hugged each other after the long summer. People waved and shouted across the masses, but nobody paid any attention to me—even the policemen. I might as well have been invisible. By the time I had decided that it was okay to go in, the halls were practically empty. There were three large tables in the foyer. Each had a sign indicating a grade level from seven to nine. I went up to the seventh-grade table.

"Name?" Asked the lady behind the table.

"Patricia Diane Greene," I whispered.

She looked up at me over her half-glasses. "Well, Miss

Greene," she said, "I believe you are in Mr. Samuelson's room. That would be room 207. Take the stairs behind me to the second floor. Turn right and go all the way to the end."

Loud bells started going off and people began to scurry, but I took my time climbing those stairs.

There were two entrances to room 207 and I took the second one that led to the back of the classroom. A short, round man with his shirt opened and his sleeves rolled up was standing at the head of the classroom reading the roll.

"You must be Patricia Greene," he said with a smile. "Come on in and find a seat."

Everyone in that room turned around to stare. Some even stood on chairs to get a better look. My eyes dropped to the floor.

"That's okay," I said, "I'll just stand back here."

A boy with red hair laughed. "Yeah, that's where the niggers are supposed to be—in the back."

Mr. Samuelson turned beet red and slammed down his attendance book. "I heard that and I will not tolerate that kind of language in my classroom.

"Miss Greene, I want you to come and sit in the front row. I want you to sit in the front, because you are going to help us make history this day. If it wasn't for your bravery, this day would be just like any other. If it were not for you, the other people in this classroom would have no idea what being a colored person is all about. You are here to make a difference for us, and I for one thank you."

"For just as the body is one and has many members, and all the members of the body, though many, are one body, so it is with Christ. For in the one Spirit we were all baptized into one body—Jews or Greeks, slaves or free—and we were all made to drink of one Spirit. Indeed, the body does not consist of one member but of many."

1 Corinthians 12:12–14

By 1961, the sit-ins and freedom rides were well under way further South and I was a senior in high school.

The Western High School was an exclusive downtown public school for girls with serious academic standards. Senior class officers and students with averages above ninety were given the privilege of having lunch at downtown restaurants. I was a class officer. (I wanted to be president, but since that would have been impossible for a Negro—we were Negroes by then—I had to run for the second most powerful job—treasurer.)

Shortly after the term had begun, everyone eligible for the senior privilege was assembled in the vice-principal's office and given a list of approved restaurants. I remember looking at the list and almost flipping out. Seven of the restaurants were segregated!

I shot a look over at Jill Collins, the only other Negro in the room, but she wouldn't give me eye contact. I quietly tucked the paper into my notebook and after school, I marched up the street to the offices of the *Afro-American Newspaper*.

The *"Afro"* was a biweekly publication and the city editor had just been named the first Negro to the school board. It took a while to convince the receptionist that Betty Moss was the only one I would talk to and it was a very curious city editor who watched me come into her office.

"What can I do for you?" she asked, shifting the papers around on her crowded desk.

"Read this," I demanded and slammed the page down in front of her.

"What is it?"

"A list of restaurants that are approved for Western High School seniors."

"So?"

"Read it," I said again, "please."

She raised her eyebrows at me and leaned back in her

chair. Suddenly she sat upright. "Some of these places are seg-regated!"

"Exactly," I said, finally sitting down.

Betty Moss smiled. "Okay," she said. "But it is one thing to think that a place is segregated and something else to be able to prove it."

I swallowed hard.

"What I need you to do," she continued, "is to get a group of friends together, go around to these restaurants, and be re-fused service. Now you don't have to get arrested or any-thing—just sign a statement that says you were not served at such-and-such a restaurant on such-and-such a date. Do you think you could do that?"

Fear was setting in. "I guess so."

"Good," she said. "Be sure to pick people that you can trust. It would be nice if it were a racially mixed group. Could you manage that?

"Yes."

"Great. Come back when that's done and we'll decide what to do next. Don't worry, I won't mention your name so you won't get in trouble with your teachers or anything."

I hadn't even thought about that, but it was too late to turn back.

I selected my trusty band of crusaders and we planned our first attack on an establishment right across from the school called The Little Restaurant.

I couldn't wait to see the inside of that place. For years I had watched my classmates disappear in The Little Restaurant af-ter school for a coke. I had never been able to join them.

It turned out to be nothing but a "greasy spoon" with a long counter and little Formica tables.

To be sure no one saw us, we had waited until long after the school's extracurricular activities were over. By then the only people in the whole place were a tired-looking woman in a dirty pink waitress uniform and a guy in work clothes drinking a cup of coffee. They were laughing and talking to each other over the counter, but they froze when we walked in.

There were seven or eight of us and we pulled two of the little tables together. It seemed like things would remain at a standoff until my friend, Kitty Stein, raised her hand to signal the waitress. The woman rolled her eyes, grabbed her order pad, and sauntered over to Kitty.

"Whaddaya want?"

"I'll have a coke," said Kitty and looked at me. "What are you having?"

"I ain't serving her," said the waitress.

"Why not?" asked Kitty.

"Policy."

"I'd like to speak to the manager," said Kitty.

"Wait a minute," said the waitress, and she disappeared into the kitchen.

Most of us were ready to bolt out of the door when she came back with this hard-looking character in a filthy apron and a T-shirt with a pack of Camel cigarettes rolled up in his sleeve.

"Y'all better get out of here before I call the po-lice," he said wiping his hands on his apron. "This here is private property and we got us a policy that says we don't have to serve no niggers. Now are you going to get out of here or do I have to get the cops to drag you out?"

"We'll be happy to leave as soon as we sign this paper," I said quickly.

"I ain't signing nothing," said the man.

"Oh no sir, you don't have to." My hands were shaking as I wrote my name and passed the sheet on.

Back on the sidewalk, we collapsed into each other's arms. In less than three days, I was back in Betty Moss's office with my mission completed.

"Very good," she said. "I'll take over from here."

That was a Thursday. On Friday evening, the *Afro-American* came out with a headline that read, "Western High School Officials Endorse Segregation."

There was a bulletin board at the front entrance to the school that was labeled "Western in the News." The idea was that articles about graduates getting married or going abroad would be posted there, but when I got to school on Monday morning, somebody had posted that article.

No sooner had I gotten to my homeroom than an announcement came over the public address system. "All students with senior privileges are asked to report to the vice-principal's office immediately."

Miss Weber was so angry she couldn't say anything, so the principal, Miss Blackiston, did all the talking. She went on and on about how shocked she was that anyone would scandalize such a fine institution while Miss Weber glared at Jill and then at me.

Well, I want you to know, I could have won an academy award for my performance. I was shocked, I was dismayed. I sighed and held my chest, fluttered my eyelids and rolled my eyes. How indeed could anyone have done such a thing to the wonderful Western High School for whom we all would gladly pledge our lives?

As it turned out, Miss Blackiston and Miss Weber were so frustrated and angry that rather than appear to concede by removing the seven from the list, they decided that the only solution was to take away the entire privilege.

"Beloved, do not be surprised at the fiery ordeal that is taking place among you to test you, as though something strange were happening to you. But rejoice insofar as you are sharing Christ's sufferings, so that you may also be glad and shout for joy when his glory is revealed. . . . For the time has come for judgment to begin with the household of

God; if it begins with us, what will be the end for those who
do not obey the gospel of God?"

1 Peter 4:12–13,17

After the first taste of "the movement," I became an addict.
I joined the Student Nonviolent Coordinating Committee
and was out marching and picketing on a regular basis. I
was arrested almost weekly, but since I was under age, I was
always released into my father's custody.

Finally, my father warned me that my demonstrating
would have to stop. I was irate—segregation would have to
stop, not me. Then my father explained that because he was
a presidential appointee to the Post Office Department in
Washington, D.C., the FBI had been keeping a file on him.
J. Edgar Hoover was not taking kindly to all these civil rights
activities, and if I kept it up, chances were that my father
could lose his job, if not worse.

I kept my promise to stay away from any demonstrations
for almost a year. It was the spring of 1963. I was a freshman
at Bennett College in Greensboro, North Carolina. Bennett is
a small "finishing" type college for black women and Greensboro was a major pulse point of the protest. The first sit-in
took place at the lunch counter of Woolworth's on Market
Street. Jesse Jackson, who attended the school now known as
North Carolina Agricultural and Technical State University,
was an emerging student leader, and the youngest of the original four sit-in demonstrators, Ezell Blair, was a senior there.

It was Ezell who had urged a group of us to attend a rally
where a nationally known leader, James Farmer from the
Congress of Racial Equity (CORE) was scheduled to speak. I
could no longer resist and in no time at all I was sucked back
into the movement like an ice cream soda through a straw.

In May of 1963 I was arrested for blocking a fire exit at the
A&S Cafeteria. Actually all I did was stand at the front door
for two seconds, but I was incarcerated for five days.

That was the whole idea. In three more days, the total number jailed was well over 900. Student leaders, including Jesse and Ezell, had developed a strategy designed to cost the city of Greensboro a great deal of money—and it did. So much so that the sheriff's people worked very hard to get us out of jail.

Our "jail" was an abandoned polio hospital with wards that stuck out from a common hallway like fat fingers on a skinny hand. Each ward included three walls of high, unshaded windows that let in whatever light was available. I was among the group arrested early in the process and so we were "lucky" to have fifteen undersized hospital beds for 120-plus women. There were three toilets, one of which worked, and two shower stalls, neither of which worked. The only privacy from our all-male guards was a series of sheets which we managed to hang across the entrance to the ward with bobby pins and hair clips.

Initially, the Sheriff simply asked us to leave, assuring everyone that our attorneys were negotiating with city representatives. We didn't believe him.

Then a rumor was spread around that A&T, which was a state school, would lose its funding. The A&T women in our ward considered this a real possibility, but the Bennett women talked them out of it. This back-and-forth business of leaving or not leaving went on for days. I had become one of the "pep people" who attempted to keep the morale up by doing things like singing freedom songs and organizing games.

By the fourth day we were nearing exhaustion. Sleeping in shifts of seven in a bed was not working. The weather had turned cold and rainy but we had given our blankets to the men in another ward who had been trying to sleep on a bare floor. The level of energy and enthusiasm had fallen to a dangerous low. My voice was so strained, I could hardly talk. Boredom had set in and tempers were on edge. On the evening of that fourth day, everyone was doing her best to help the time pass—playing cards, doing each other's hair, snoozing, studying—when all of a sudden there was glass breaking all around us.

The men from the neighboring wards came crashing through the windows. Someone had told them that we were being attacked and raped by the guards. They shouted at us to find protection. Thinking that the guards would not hurt women, we scurried to block the aisles. We held our bodies in the protective position we had been taught in nonviolent seminars, while the men dove for the beds.

But it was too late. The guards came in swinging their clubs and hitting at everything. People screamed. Some prayed out loud. Others sang. Men were dragged through the aisles. Blood and noise were everywhere—and then there was nothing.

With no time between the removal of the men and our ability to think rationally, the sheriff announced that the A&T women would have to return to school or be permanently expelled. This time the Bennett women could not convince them otherwise. The next morning, they were gone.

The president of our college, Dr. Willa B. Player, came to the abandoned hospital to tell us how proud everyone was of us, but now it was time to consider our safety. She said it was up to us, but there were no longer enough people to make a difference and we were vulnerable. The vote was to give up.

It was raining that afternoon. Rides had been arranged to take us back to campus, but the restaurants, theaters, and laundromats still would not admit "Negroes." I remember looking back at the sheriff as I crossed the parking lot. He smiled and touched his hat.

> "Deliver me , O LORD, from evildoers;
> protect me from those who are violent,
> who plan evil things in their minds
> and stir up wars continually.
> Guard me, O LORD, from the hands of the wicked;

protect me from the violent
who have planned my downfall."
Psalm 140:1–2, 4

My experiences in Greensboro came to the attention of my sorority and I was elected to a national committee on social action. And so it was that I found myself walking the streets of Watts in Los Angeles in 1965 one week after the first time there were riots—the first time anger and frustration had turned into burning, violence, and looting.

Through the efforts of our leaders and others, community people, politicians, and philanthropists were brought together. The conversations were good and it was with a feeling of accomplishment that we witnessed the understanding developing from those dialogues. It was with pride that we heard the promises to begin working on solutions to the problems that had erupted into violence.

The vision was that in twenty years economic development in the area would enable the marginalized society to merge into the mainstream. Twenty-seven years later, I watched Watts burn all over again on big screen TV and I wept.

There is certainly more I could tell you. I could describe the magic and promise that surrounded the March on Washington—the words of Reverend King and the music of Mahalia Jackson. I could tell you about the time of King's assassination when I was very pregnant and we lived in Baltimore. I could tell you how frightened Tom was to leave our home because we had been pelted with rocks by other black people as we drove through Walbrook Junction, where the fires burned and the looters ran free.

I could tell you more, but enough is enough. Enough is enough.

"I consider that the sufferings of this present time are not worth comparing with the glory about to be revealed to us.

For the creation waits with eager longing for the revealing of the children of God; . . . We know that the whole creation has been groaning in labor pains until now; and not only the creation, but we ourselves, who have the first fruits of the Spirit, groan inwardly while we wait for adoption, the redemption of our bodies. For in hope we were saved. Now hope that is seen is not hope. For who hopes for what is seen? But if we hope for what we do not see, we wait for it with patience."

Romans 8:18–19, 22–25

O merciful and gracious God,
Grant us continued hope that we may have the patience to wait for that great day of understanding whenever it comes.

Lord, we know about hatred, but on this day in which we celebrate the life of your remarkable servant, Martin Luther King, Jr., teach us to recognize the unconditional love of Christ.

Teach us to love those who do not think as we do. Teach us to love the unlovable who thrive on hatred, and allow us to help them find peace. Help us to understand our neighbors and hear their point of view with a love that will lead us to the world that you would like for us to be.

And most of all Dear Lord, guide our hearts and minds that we may keep hope alive. In Jesus' name we pray. Amen.

In Your Own Words

A Million Men Marching

Isaiah 65:17–25; 40:28–31,
2 Thessalonians 3:6–13

A million men marching or a million marching men? A million marching men or a million men marching?

Listen to this:

> Let me give you a word on the philosophy of reform. The whole history of the progress of human liberty shows that all concessions yet made to her august claims have been born of earnest struggle. The conflict has been exciting, agitating, all absorbing, and for the time being putting all other tumult to silence. It must do this or it does nothing. If there is no struggle there is no progress. Those who profess to favor freedom, and yet deprecate agitation, are men who want crops without plowing up the ground. They want rain without thunder and lightning. They want the ocean without the awful roar of its many waters. This struggle may be a moral one; or it may be a physical one; or it may be both moral and physical; but it must be a struggle. Power concedes nothing without a demand. It never did and it never will.

Those were the words of Frederick Douglass in 1853.

Marching men follow a leader. Men marching champion a cause.

Once we lived in villages where the highly respected elders guided the life of the community with fairness and folk wisdom. Once we lived in a place where everyone took responsibility for the education and well-being of children. Adolescents went through a conscientious process to learn about adulthood and the values of life. There was a ceremony when those lessons were learned and a celebration when a teen became an adult. We have lost the pride of Africa and a new pride must emerge for Afro-America.

Hear the words of Isaiah 65:17–18: "For I am about to create new heavens and a new earth; the former things shall not be remembered or come to mind. But be glad and rejoice forever in what I am creating . . ."

A million men MARCHING.

What panic must have flourished in the hearts of the powerful men when it was proposed that one million of the most powerless in this country would come together to march in the nation's capitol.

Typically, these million men were not the glib, altruistic, college-educated, middle class civil rights marchers of 1963. These million men were painfully familiar with racism and classism. These million men had an intimate knowledge of violence both as victims and as perpetrators. These men did not shy away from the physical, they lived by it.

The powerful attempted to disrupt this marching by inciting a friction between the men and the women. "Why just men?" they asked.

The answer points to a beginning in slavery when men were sold away from their wives and children from their parents. By necessity, women moved away from the patriarchal model of their African heritage and became the backbone of whatever collection of people could be considered family— black or white, through biology or because of proximity.

What follows is a history of limited "privilege" and subsequent family control for the black female. The black male's perceived brute strength and prowess has traditionally been too much of a threat for the powerful—the white American male.

Hence, it is easier for those in power to maintain their positions of power by doing whatever necessary to keep others—particularly men of color—from taking over. For African Americans this has historically included providing more educational opportunities and occupational advancements for the black female.

The other thing about slavery is that it forced the black man into thinking that earning a living meant working for somebody else, and that is what it still means for many today. The entrepreneurial spirit of self-employment frequently found among other racial ethnic groups is strangely absent or limited in Afro-Americans.

These circumstances combined with assorted other reasons from racism to a welfare system that penalizes families with fathers living in the home, results in what we see today—the black man typically at the bottom of the socio-economic success heap.

True, we are speaking in generalities and, of course, there are exceptions. But is it any wonder that so many of our African sons and lifemates, fathers and brothers are frustrated, angry, and disappointed with the mainstream of American life?

And what happens to all this frustration, anger, and disappointment? It cannot be directed at the mainstream. (Although there have been the crazies who have tried. Remember the man who opened fire on the New York commuter train?)

All of this frustration, anger, and disappointment tends to float until it finds a substitute target. It beats up on women, abandons children, helps itself to anything it wants, and flirts with self-destruction. Most African American women welcomed an opportunity for their men to feel good about who they are and to give recognition to the gifts they have to give.

In Isaiah 40:29, we read, "He gives power to the faint, and

strengthens the powerless." *Strength* to the powerless—not power to the powerless, but *strength*. The power comes from within. God releases that power with the strength of the Holy Spirit. With faith and trust in God, come faith and trust in self through the intervention of the Holy Spirit. Remember how those dry bones were given flesh, but needed the Holy Spirit for the breath of new life?

With belief in God comes belief in one's own ability to manage whatever life dishes out. With God, the challenges of life become life's opportunities. With God's energy and without weariness, each and every one has the power to strive and overcome, to let go or let God.

A million MEN marching.

What panic must have flourished in the hearts of the powerful when it was proposed that one million of the most powerless would come together to march on the capitol, the center of power in this country. What panic there must have been when they learned that the one bringing these million men together was one who has been continuously stung by hatred and who has continuously spewed back that hatred's venom.

But he said he came by God's direction. He said God wanted him to gather these million men—the most alienated, disenfranchised group among America's teeming masses yearning to be free. God told him to help these million men demonstrate their unity and strength by peacefully marching in political protest of the social, educational, and economic opportunities they have traditionally been denied.

Now we know that Farrakhan's history is not without racist and violent blemishes, but are we to miss the message because of the messenger? Farrakhan said what needed to be said and what needed to be heard by those gathered: African American men, you are the children of God. You are lovable and worthwhile. Worship your God, take responsibility for your children, and stop killing each other.

Perhaps, there is no other group that God would need to call together for such a message. Yet, for many of these million, accepting Christ's charge to "love thy neighbor as thyself" means that they must first love themselves.

Some folks felt that Farrakhan's message was too obvious to warrant all the money that went into travel and new clothes. And yes, that money could have been well spent on the children of these men.

Yet, I can't help remembering the response from Jesus when Judas made a similar complaint about money spent on expensive oils instead of the poor. Jesus said the poor will always be with you, but I won't. How many times will a million African American men gather in unity?

Listen to Isaiah 12:1: "You will say in that day: I will give thanks to you, O LORD, for though you were angry with me, your anger turned away, and you comforted me."

A MILLION men, marching.

The powerful said there really weren't a million men. Maybe there were and maybe there were not. The point is the masses were there to hear, "to be lifted up on the wings of eagles," to spread the awesome feeling of pride to the brothers who were not at that place.

The future will come with the rippling water of direction and self-motivation. The dream will be realized when the children no longer wonder what it would be like to have a Daddy, when the body temples are no longer polluted with debilitating drugs, when the minds are clear to focus on the healing salve of forgiveness.

The powerful warned that so many black men together would cause a safety problem, and those in attendance would be participating at their own risk even though additional police and national guard protection were to be provided. But there was no violence.

"They will not hurt or destroy on all my holy mountain; for

the earth will be full of the knowledge of the LORD as the waters cover the sea" (Isa. 11:9).

The powerful urged other black leaders to denounce the march and its creator, Louis Farrakhan, but instead they vowed to support the cause. If you truly believe in and identify with Afro-America, there is no way to turn your back on a movement that will affirm those who have never felt affirmed, that will strengthen those who have never felt strong.

Even Colin Powell, teased with the prospect of preeminence among the powerful—or should I say, especially Colin Powell—took a dedicated political risk publicly to endorse the cause of the march. He did not attend because he dared not take a greater risk—the risk of losing the possibility of carrying his brothers, on his own shoulders, to a new plateau of promise. Could it be the eagle wings of a general that will send us soaring?

We can only wait for the Lord's chosen time, "but those who wait for the LORD shall renew their strength, they shall mount up with wings like eagles, they shall run and not be weary, they shall walk and not faint" (Isa. 40:31).

The powerful could not deny that the march was impressive, and with a few more swipes at the leadership, the event was declared over. But African Americans cannot afford to stop marching. The descendants of Ham must continue to prepare for the role God will give them when the time is right and they are ready. Self-empowerment is crucial to that readiness.

We must urge those million to continue marching, to spread the pride of a new man of color, all over the United States. Together, we must bring more brothers and sisters to the commitment of healthy relationship and dedicated responsibility to family in Afro-America.

And for those who do not embrace the cause, for those who refuse to recognize the promise of God for them, what will become of them? For those who continue to ignore the women they impregnate and the children they father, what can be done? For those who depend on violence for self-validation, for those whose lives are supported by crime, what shall be their final reward?

Listen to Paul's second letter to the Thessalonians 3:13–14: "Brothers and sisters, do not be weary in doing what is right. Take note of those who do not obey what we say . . . have nothing to do with them, so that they may be ashamed. Do not regard them as enemies, but warn them as believers."

The message is clear. We are not to condemn, but neither are we to condone. While we accept those who refuse to turn their lives around as our brothers and sisters, we do not accept their behavior as admirable, appropriate, or appreciated. We can only pray that somehow they will discover God's love for them and use it as a shield against all the evils that tempt them.

In the meantime, we must do whatever we can to encourage each other, to applaud our accomplishments no matter how small, and pray for God's continued strength and energy that those million men marching, and those of us at home support-ing them, will rise up on the wings of eagles to soar to the heights of self-empowerment, peace, and prosperity for everyone.

Gracious God,

We give you thanks. Thanks for the gift of life and the gift of liv-ing. We ask that you continue to hold us up on your mighty wings that we may soar to that new day of heaven and earth.

And dear Lord, we pray that you bless the men of Genesis in their efforts to save those sinking into an abyss of uselessness to them-selves and others.

Lord, we thank you for the spirit of the million men who marched and for the million men such as the men of Genesis, who were not able to attend, but embrace your spirit in tireless energy.

Dear God, we are grateful for those who have worked so hard and long that this important mission not be lost.

We ask that you guide them to new days of accomplishment and peaceful nights of rest.

These things we ask in the name of Jesus the Christ, who died that we may live life to our fullest potential. Amen.

In Your Own Words

Uppity Women Who Can't Find Their Place

Genesis 21:8–21 and Matthew 10:24–31

About Glass Ceilings

Those who know me well can imagine my reaction when I read the lectionary text from Genesis. A black woman with an attitude—could I relate or what? I delved into the research and was amazed to see books written around this one little passage.

Hagar was an Egyptian slave girl who was exclusively the handmaiden to Sarah, who was the wife of Abram and head of a very wealthy household. It is easy to imagine that Hagar probably fancied herself above the other slaves because of her close relationship with Sarah. (It was a house slave versus field slave kind of thing.) Plus, Sarah had been very careful not to allow Hagar to be used for sexual favors as were others in the household.

Therefore, when it looked like Sarah could not have children herself, it seemed like a good idea to offer Hagar's virgin purity to her husband. And, as per their culture, Sarah, as Hagar's owner, would be considered the child's mother.

However, as can be the case in many modern surrogate mother situations, people get emotionally confused. Hagar figured that she had accomplished what Sarah could not. She had become a wife to Abram and conceived a child. Since fertility was the primary measure of a woman's worth in that time, Hagar felt she should replace the incompetent first wife.

Notice the appearance of what we have come to call "glass ceilings." They are those boundaries that are not visible until they obstruct attempts to rise above them. "Glass ceilings" tend to be constructed by those in power to prevent those not in power from "re-placing" them. Glass ceilings are designed to define another person's station or "place" in the scheme of things, such as women in corporate worlds who may rise to vice presidencies, but no further.

Regardless of her competence and qualifications, Hagar was a black female. By tradition and social order, she was not "supposed" to attain Sarah's place.

So, what do you do when God has blessed you with gifts and talents, but the people in power are too insecure to let you use them?

Sometimes, you work around it.

Back in the 1960s, when I was in a predominantly white, all girl's high school, I knew there was no way that I could be elected as president of the class. Although I felt I had the leadership skills to do a better job than the others running, I was a black student in a city below the Mason-Dixon line. I won easily as treasurer and was able to keep those in power accountable in ways they had not expected.

At other times, God has called me to test the glass ceiling, push against it, or break it—even though the shattering glass would cause injury and pain.

Some know the story of my involvement in the integrating of my junior high school in compliance with the Supreme Court decision. They have heard me speak of the time in Greensboro when I was incarcerated during the civil rights movement. They remember that I was the first African American woman to moderate the Presbytery of Cincinnati and I did so at a time of great turbulence.

God called me again. This time to be a candidate for Moderator of the General Assembly of the Presbyterian Church (U.S.A.) in 1997. God called me at a time when affirmative action practices in the church had been challenged, when mission dollars for programs that ease the lives of minorities were being cut from mission budgets. God called me at a time when a contingency of African Americans wanted to secede from the denomination, when major theological differences among Presbyterians continued to resist compromise. God called me at a time when the Presbyterian church was facing bankruptcy and black churches were routinely burned to the ground.

It has been several years since the Presbyterian Church (U.S.A.) has trusted an African American to be its moderator. I was frightened, but God's call was strong.

Did Hagar realize the risk she was taking by challenging Sarah or did she simply ignore the obvious? In either case, Hagar's "uppity attitude" did not sit well with Sarah, who went directly to Abram and proceeded to blame him. Then, as husbands often do with enraged wives, Abram threw up his hands and said, "Sarah, she's your slave, do whatever you want."

Sarah was brutal and Hagar took off. Can't you just see it? Girlfriend with hand on her hip? "I didn't ask for this mess, and I don't have to put up with it!"

Enter an angel of God who confronts Hagar on the road. You see God wanted Hagar to do something else with her life and, make no mistake, you can never run away from what God has in mind.

"Where did you come from and where are you going?" asked the angel.

Hagar's answer was quick. "Away from my mistress." You can hear her adding something like, "That woman has lost her mind. I ain't staying around for her to beat up on like some animal, etc., etc." But what Hagar suddenly realized was that she had no plan and no place to go.

The angel offered her a deal. Hagar was promised a son whom she was to name Ishmael, which means "God hears." If she went back, her descendants would be "too numerous to be counted." It was a promise that Hagar could not refuse. It offered her hope and immortality.

But the promise had a second clause that some say explains the plight of the black man throughout history. Ishmael would be a "wild donkey of a man," meaning he would live outside of the villages of society. Genesis 16:12 reads, ". . . with his hand against everyone, and everyone's hand against him; and he shall live at odds with all his kin."

Saving Our Sons

Genesis 21 brings us back into the story about sixteen years later. Ishmael is a teenager. Sarah has conceived in her old age and given birth to Isaac, who has just been weaned.

Apparently, Ishmael is crazy about little Isaac and spends a lot of time playing with him. Watching them, it occurs to Sarah that they are brothers and Ishmael is the firstborn. Custom could work against Isaac's favored status. Abraham is an old man and if something were to happen to him, Ishmael could inherit all of Abraham's fortunes, which were considerable.

So Sarah goes back to Abraham and complains. This time she demands that the slave woman and the slave woman's son be expelled from the household at once. Special emphasis was probably made on the "slave" part to remind Abraham of Hagar's place in the scheme of things.

Well, Abraham wasn't real comfortable with this. After all, Ishmael was the man's son! So Abraham talks to God about it and God assures him that everything is under control. The two will be cared for. Reassured, Abraham gives Hagar some bread and something to drink and sends them off into the desert.

So what happens when they go off into the "wilderness"? The only thing we can be certain of is that nobody takes them in—which is curious since, once again, such was the custom. Is there a possibility of discrimination or is Hagar being uppity and insisting that she can handle things by herself?

Delores Williams centers an entire theology on this aspect of the story. The analogy is amazing. In her book *Sisters in the Wilderness*, Williams points out that Hagar and Ishmael are a model of many African American families with one single parent/head of household. You have a woman, struggling alone, venturing into the world to scratch out a living for herself and her child in spite of the poverty that "ruling-class economics" has consigned to them.

Continuing the comparison, let's look at a book by Marita Golden, who is best known for her novels. However, *Saving Our Sons* is an autobiographical account of her experience as a single parent raising an African American son in today's world of stereotypical attitudes and black-on-black violence. In speaking of what her son must endure, Golden writes, "Michael would inhabit that narrow, corrupt crawl space in the minds of whites and some black people too, a space reserved for criminals, outcasts, misfits, and black men. Soon he would become a permanent suspect." Movingly, she goes on to talk about the women who will hesitate to get into an elevator with him, the police who will watch him more closely, and the store owners who would have their security guards follow him around.

My cousin's twenty-two-year-old son was traveling on a train from Philadelphia to Toronto to attend a family celebration. The train was detained at the Canadian border by police and customs officials. Although there had been a drug trafficking tip, this young man was the only one removed to another car, searched, and interrogated for almost a half hour. He was also the only black person on the train.

Could it be that many minority race youngsters are "programmed" by prejudgment? How many decide not to try because they are expected to fail anyway? How many who see their friends and relatives survive by stealing and violence decide that such behavior is the only way to go? Ishmael developed skill with a bow and arrow in a land where people pillaged to survive.

Consider the mind that can organize a twenty-four-hour product delivery system including the specific scheduling of personnel. Does the innate intelligence and skill change when the product is illegal and the mind probably didn't graduate from high school?

So what's a mother to do?

Marita Golden tells the story of a woman who could have been a modern-day Hagar. "Ella Ross is a tiny woman of impressive self-possession, and it was clear soon after I met her that her emotional investment in her son was the singular and most important force in her life." Her son was the chance to erase the horrors of her own childhood and somehow attain a certain kind of grace.

Ella Ross's son, Terence Brown, was a gifted writer, a star athlete, and an honor roll scholar who had been easily accepted into college. When Terence was arrested for the murder of a police officer, it was believed to be a case of mistaken identity, much like the case of my cousin on the train.

But as the evidence was collected and the trial evolved, it became apparent that the lure of the streets had been too great. Golden wondered if all the confidence that his mother had bestowed on Terence had given him a sense of invincibility, a false notion that he could rob or kill and go off to college the next morning. The lawyer told Golden he has seen many Terences. He said they always come into his office with their mothers, never their fathers. He said that the mothers always want him to talk to their sons the way some man should have talked to them long before. But by then it is too late.

African American women seem to be expected to lead the

race out of bondage, but the fact is they cannot do it alone. What can the church do?

We could start by reaching out to families like Hagar and Ishmael or Ella and Terence. And not only could we offer the services of the Caring Place, we could welcome them into our fellowship, give them responsibility in the life of the congregation, and let them share in the ownership of our worship experiences.

It wasn't so long ago that the Mission & Outreach Committee of my church had a wonderful proposal for teens-at-risk in the neighborhood. We were going to provide a safe haven for studying and being together in the after-school hours. We were going to find computers they could learn on, telephones they could use in privacy, and TV/videos that they could watch. The proposal was not funded by the city, but does that mean we should give up? We won't be able to save everybody, but we may save one and that will make all the effort worthwhile.

Letting Go to Let God

But what happens when it's too late? What do all the "uppity women" like Ella Ross do when their hope is sentenced to life in prison or even death? What did Hagar do, alone in the wilderness with no food or water and the hope for her son near death? What can any parent do when they cannot find the way to pull their children from the jaws of violence, from the quicksand of drugs, from the precipice of depression and low self-esteem, from the briars of disease?

Hagar was near the end. She placed her son's body under a bush and, knowing he would die, she walked away because she could not bear to watch. Seated on a rock some distance away, all she could do was cry.

I know that kind of crying. It wrenches your insides and plays havoc with your soul. The tears do not stop. They pour down your cheeks like something has gone haywire with the basic plumbing. You take deep breaths, you blow your nose—but nothing changes, nothing will make the tears stop until you remember there is a higher power who loves you, until you let go so God can take over.

Jesus said, "Are not two sparrows sold for a penny? Yet not one of them will fall to the ground apart from your Father. And even the hairs of your head are all counted. So do not be afraid; you are of more value than many sparrows" (Matt. 10:29–31). Why does it take so long for us to remember God? Is this an off-shoot of our pride? Do we really believe we have all the answers? Are we actually convinced that we can do it all?

The fact is that Hagar never did ask for God's help. It was Ishmael. God heard and gave the angel instructions for Hagar to save her son.

Are we waiting for someone else to ask?

Magnificent Protector God,
We are worried. We are worried for our children, those you have entrusted to us when they are young and those that surround us in the streets.

Help us to know, Lord, when we can act before it is too late, and help us to know when we must accept whatever comes. Give us the strength to let go when it is your will and hold us in the power of your love as we pass the control to you. For ultimately, we know you are in charge of all of our lives and we try to accept that it is your will that shall prevail.

Teach us to understand our pride as Christians, and show us how to use that pride to further your mission on earth.

Loving Spirit, lead us to the place at your table where we belong together as sisters and brothers of Jesus the Christ.

We ask these things in his name. Amen.

In Your Own Words

MEDITATIONS

Praying for the People

"He leads the humble in what is right,
and teaches the humble his way.
All the paths of the LORD are steadfast love
    and faithfulness. . . .
Redeem Israel, O God, out of all its troubles."
                        Psalm 25:9–10, 22

"Humility" and "American politics" have moved to opposite ends of the spectrum. It doesn't matter whether we are
talking Democrats, Republicans, or Independents, humility
surfaces only as a stance for campaign ads. Congress, the President, and even the Supreme Court love to work the word
"God" into their public speeches, but you have to wonder how
often the name passes over their lips in private.

Politics is no longer about providing fair and accountable
government for the people. It has become an out-of-control
game of "Who's Got the Power?" The rule is there are no
rules. Faithfulness and loyalty is to the party, not the country.
Accountability is to the opinion polls and the media reporters.
The key is to focus on the buzz words. The good ones end with
"reform." The bad ones use "control."

The "mud-slinging" campaigns, the dirty tricks that justify
the end rather than the means, the irreversible filthy pollu-
tion of character and successful programs, the media's digging only for sensational scum and discovering it among the

148

"plants," has soiled our entire system of government from Washington on down. American politics needs a bath. The United States of America needs to have its "feet plucked from the net of its enemies" within.

We have to vote with ballot and voice. We have to take responsibility for who can "decide what is best for us." We have to insist on what is right rather than what gets the party elected. We have to divorce partisan politics and consider the best interest of the whole. We have to pray that leadership will find the path of the Lord, the steadfast fullness and love for others as much as for themselves.

Omnipotent God,
We are grateful to live in the wealthiest, most powerful country in the world. But Lord, our country is in trouble. Help us to return to the principles of decency, honor, selflessness, humility, and love in the way we govern ourselves and the people who govern us. Amen.

"The LORD judges the peoples;
judge me, O LORD, according to my righteousness
and according to the integrity that is in me."

Psalm 7:8

Martin Luther King, Jr., had a dream that people would be judged "not by the color of their skin, but by the content of their character." The psalmist had a similar hope. A hope that the people of Israel would not be falsely accused by the powerful simply because they were people of Israel.

A black person running is fleeing a crime. A white person running is jogging. A wallet is stolen at a predominantly white private school and planted in the locker of an African American student on scholarship. The scholarship student is expelled because the authorities never questioned their personal assumptions. More than one black man standing on a corner indicates they are dealing drugs. More than one white man and they are waiting for a ride. A well-dressed black woman, with grandchild in tow, is followed around the store to be sure she does not steal the merchandise. Her white counterpart is offered a credit card.

These examples are exactly why the O. J. Simpson verdict was so popular among many African Americans: He was assumed innocent because of a shadow of a doubt rather than guilty because of the "shadow" of his skin color. For most, the victory was less about the murder of two people, than a weakened link in the ongoing character assassination of a people.

The tragedy of subtle "prejudgments" is the societal buy-in. And society includes African Americans. A phenomenon named "white privilege" by scholars is a cultural stance that becomes an acceptable rule of thumb, if one is not paying attention. Case in point: Two people arrive at a cash register at exactly the same time. The white person is waited on first and sometimes by a black person. Why is this? Because of our country's history of slavery, the European American is deemed superior and therefore "privileged." For many people, this type of "white privilege" is a habit rather than an opinion. But it is a habit that can be easily altered if we program ourselves to be alert to such situations.

Pointing out who really should be waited on—"She can be first," or "I believe that person was ahead of me"—is a simple action that affirms the other person in a not-so-simple way. We can tell children that everyone is the same, but until this bears out in the everyday world, they will never own that truth.

Those of us requiring affirmation have more to do. Black and/or female, we have to rid ourselves of the notion that somebody else is better or can do something better because they are white and/or male. It is a tough assignment to reverse what we have been "taught" about our lack of value, but God is our refuge and our shield and our judge—our only judge.

Defender God,
Be with me to affirm my worth, especially at those times when I too
may question it. Strengthen my integrity when it is questioned. Help
me to be judged righteous because I am striving to be more like your
son, Jesus Christ. Amen.

"Now we know
that the law is good,
if one uses it legitimately."
1 Timothy 1:8

Our society has developed a basic distrust of laws and law-makers. Lawyer jokes have become the fastest-growing body of humor in the Western world. The sense is that law has become comedy. (Funny how folks with the most money "fair" better in the court system than those with the least.)

Could law be synonymous with justice? Apparently not to the extent that we would like. Paul suggests that this may be due to not using the law legitimately. Let's explore that in our world.

Acts of violence are not committed by any morally clear-thinking, rational individual. Does that mean that the law can be twisted so that anyone committing a violent crime is insane—temporarily or otherwise—and therefore should be excused?

Could law be synonymous with public safety or would that translate into the government's prescribing only the foods that are good for us? Does it mean that a person should be penalized for an unhealthy behavior such as smoking? Is Big Brother watching? Where does concern for the well-being of the public stop and infringement on individual rights begin?

The laws of God are not to limit but to identify the boundaries between right and wrong. Man has made that which was clear fuzzy.

Dear God,
Help me to understand that your laws are not there to restrict me
but to give me the borders of goodness and evil. Teach me the best
way to live within your lines. Amen.

"Therefore, whoever breaks one of the least of these commandments, and teaches others to do the same, will be called
least in the kingdom of heaven; but whoever does them and
teaches them will be called great in the kingdom of heaven."
Matthew 5:19

We are always prioritizing things in our lives. There is only so
much time in a day or money in the bank. We have to make
decisions about what is more important so that we can be certain those are the things taken care of.

The problem comes when we apply our habit of prioritizing to God's commandments. Is it really as criminal to tell a
small untruth as to kill someone? One act is punishable by
men, the other is punishable by God.

And what about the degrees of wrong that we have created
to modify God's commandments for our purposes? It is not
right to kill another human being—unless of course you are de-
fending what you believe in or the person's heinous behavior
has condemned him to death. Yet when young people slur over
such nuances in their street wars, we consider them barbaric.

What kind of messages are we giving to our children who
watch cartoon characters steal, maim, and kill? What kind of
messages are we giving to teens whose movie and music idols
openly engage in sexual relationships outside of marriage
without any apparent negative consequences?

Should we re-engage ourselves in the business of bringing
faith and a sense of morality to as many people as we can—
young and old? Should we return to applying a moral spin to

our civic and political activities? Or should the end really justify the means?

Dear God,

*I need help understanding your absolutes. I want to do right things
and I want my children to learn good from evil. Yet the permis-
siveness of what goes on around me is confusing. Guide me to your
will and forgive me when I go astray. Amen.*

".. . the people who sat in darkness have seen a great light,
and for those who sat in the region and shadow of death
light has dawned."

Matthew 4:16

What would it mean to sit in the region of death? The imme-
diate image that comes to mind could be a mental institution
where individuals are heavily medicated and lost to "normal"
living. They sit and stare or rock and make strange noises because their minds are not able to lead them through the maze
of daily living. Perhaps they are restrained to prevent them
from harming themselves or others. Perhaps they leap up to
wander around aimlessly, only to return to their chair to rock
again.

Could this be a distortion of life that is marginal enough
to "sit in the region of death"? Could our lives be just as
lost? Could we be wandering through our days just as aimlessly?

God gives meaning to life—a reason to exist, a light at the
end of a tunnel of despair. God is the medication that controls
our mental confusion. God releases us from the restraint of
depression and gives meaning to our noises.

Blessed Lord,

Turn on the lights of my life. Give it hope and enthusiasm. In many

*ways, I know what it feels like to be dying. Give me the strength and
direction to find your dawn. Amen.*

"I will show portents
in the heavens and
on earth, blood and fire
and columns of smoke."
Joel 2:30

How many times do we shake our heads at street corner
soothsayers who warn us about the end of the world? Yet here
we find a modification of that theme which may hit us pretty
close to home.

The subject is God's response to concerns regarding the
ruin of the country. (Joel is talking about Israel, but America,
the Morally Nonchalant, could be easily substituted.) The
assurance is that those who follow God will be saved. God's
spirit will be "poured out" so that sons and daughters shall
prophesy, old men shall dream dreams, and young men shall
see visions.

The question is when. The scripture says "portents in
heaven" will warn us. Could that be anything like the thunder
and lightning that happens during a January snow storm?
Could "blood" be the epidemic of war and violence that has
taken over the world? Could "fire" be the result of massive
brush fires in the United States and Australia? Could we be
talking about the smoke stacks of industry that shoot off
columns of pollutants that return to the earth as acid rain?

How close is God to reclaiming earth from the irresponsi-
bility of humans whom he placed in charge?

O God of Power and Might,
Keep me aware of your will and your majesty. Help me to prepare
myself and others for the time when you will come again. Allow me
to know your Spirit, to dream your dreams, that my days on earth
will be worthy of the gift of life that you have given me. Amen.

In Your Own Words